HOW THE

A MILLION

The Dyke & Dryden Story

by Tony Wade

with a foreword by Bill Morris

A Hansib Publication

First published in 2001 by Hansib Publications Limited
Tower House, 141-149 Fonthill Road, London N4 3HF, England

ISBN 1 870518 83 7 (Pb)
ISBN 1 870518 84 5 (Hb)

Cover designed by Graphic Resolutions, Herts

Production by Books of Colour and Graphic Resolutions

Printed by Woolnoughs, Northants

The Dyke & Dryden Story

Dedication

It is with a deep sense of pride that I dedicate this book to all past members of staff, and to all the entrepreneurs who choose to follow a business career.

Acknowledgements

MY colleagues, Len Dyke and Dudley Dryden, are men of immense vision, lending their names to a partnership which in June 1968 became a limited liability with my acquisition of one third of the equity. They were equally magnanimous in their call to rename the business, Dyke, Dryden & Wade, which I decided was unnecessary.

As a team, our skills were complementary. We shared a common philosophy, that of putting the needs of building the business above everything else. Without their vision, hard work and drive, there would be no story to tell.

I would also like to acknowledge the magnificent administrative support provided by Pearl Goodridge in the efficient management of my office. Special thanks to writer Robert Govender and consultant Christopher Johnson for their valuable advice.

Thanks also to Rudi Page of Statecraft Consulting, Clair Jackson for jogging my memory, and to my son Anthony Jnr for reading the manuscript and offering his valuable opinions.

Finally, I would like to thank my darling wife, Vasantha, for her extreme patience in reading and re-reading my manuscript and giving up so much of her quiet moments to share my ideas and help to make sense of them.

Foreword

FOR too long, there has been a perception that the Black Community's contribution to contemporary Britain is limited to the social agenda associated with the so-called race relations industry. It is refreshing therefore to traverse the history of Dyke & Dryden on their personal journey to economic liberation.

If every journey of a thousand miles starts with one small step, then the achievements chronicled by Tony Wade in this book are as relevant in distance travelled and obstacles conquered as Neil Armstrong's journey to the moon.

Any mistaken belief that equality of opportunity applies when black entrepreneurs meet white bank managers, has been soon dispelled by the Dyke & Dryden experience, which shows that black businesses are not even rated high enough to be considered for venture capital risk.

Despite these odds, the book demonstrates that the Black Community can enjoy the fruits of economic liberation by and through its own efforts. Economically liberated black people are able, like their white counterparts, to exercise choice - such as deciding where to live, which, in turn, may influence the choice made for children's schooling. Starting a virtuous circle, which challenges the dynamics of a closed society and leads to the power and influence which come with proper and full representation.

The spin-offs from the Dyke & Dryden experience are many - not least of which is the message of trust. For too long, black people in Britain have been held back through lack of trust in each other.

How else can their lack of economic progress, compared with the Jewish and that of the Ugandan Asian communities be explained. Although we started with the major advantage of a common language, somehow, save for one or two exceptions, we managed not even to be in the race.

The lessons from this book demonstrate that not only can trust be engendered between and within the Black Community, but a real partnership can be built - with the community as stakeholders.

The Dyke & Dryden model shows the difference between the long-established trickle down effect and a positive recycling of effort and resources within the community. The community supported the company and purchased its products - from records to haircare - and, in return, Dyke & Dryden promoted their needs - such as the opportunity for young black women to get a foothold on the career ladder of modelling. But the biggest gains of all were in the field of employment and skills development where many opportunities were created in the Black Community.

This book abounds with lessons for the Black Community and proves that it can be a vibrant incubator not only for knowledge but also for pride and ambition.

As I move to the concluding chapters of this book, I stop to wonder how many hopes have been dashed and how many ambitions ruined - not because they lacked the drive and determination of Dyke & Dryden, but because they paid the price of discrimination.

As we learn the lessons of success from Dyke & Dryden, let us not forget those who did not manage to stay the course. They will, I know, continue to pursue their own liberation towards social justice and economic prosperity.

I personally believe that the Dyke & Dryden experience will, within the Black Community, uncover their will to win and their vision to succeed.

Bill Morris

Contents

Dyke & Dryden
A personal reflection

LOOKING back over three decades of business and community involvement, has anything changed for the advancement of Britain's Black community? This is a question I keep asking myself.

Black business, meaning business conducted by Black people, is sometimes perceived as illegal and often confused with the term the "Black Economy". This note, simplistic as it sounds, because of an unfounded perception often presents barriers with no good reason, denying perfectly sound business propositions to get off the ground. Later on in this book I will give examples of my own experience.

Much is made of the glossy phrase of "Equal Opportunity" across the entire employment arena as a whole, but often overlooking the subtle distinction between "Equal Opportunity" and equal access.

It is this denial of equal access which makes the going so tough on the Black community, something I have been highlighting whenever the opportunity presented itself over the years.

My first serious attempt in airing my strongly held views was as chairman of the UK Caribbean Chamber of Commerce in our year-end Annual Report, volume 6, June/July 1982. An extract of that report is shown below:

It is my belief, that if we are to win the goals we set ourselves then discipline and a willingness to make some sacrifices for the good of ourselves is fundamental. The consideration should always be what can we contribute to build a strong institution that we could all be proud of, to work for us, our community and the nation.

We have succeeded in arousing national consciousness of the difficulties ethnic business people face in acquiring start up or expansion capital, and of the harm it does both in demoralising and rending to waste skills and human resources that should be gainfully employed. Lack of capital where one qualifies not only denies the right of equal opportunity, but also denies the ethnic community to develop, making itself supportive and will perpetuate poverty for generations to come. Access to capital by itself is not enough, management skills to use funds that become available go hand in hand and here again we must look to the institutions of learning to assist in preparing tailor-made programmes.

We must also appeal to the leaders in industry and commerce to give a lead in promoting people who qualify for positions of management, the outcome of which could only make for a healthier and a more harmonious society.

Where are we now? The answer is on the threshold of a great historical change and it's up to us to keep the momentum going, since the changes taking place now will profoundly affect the lives of many of us from now on.

This change calls for a sincerity of purpose, it calls for dedication, it presents us with a challenge. The way ahead is long and hard, but attainable. Sharing in the mainstream of the British economy must be our ultimate aim.

I would like to consider myself as taking a realistic stand in facing up to the difficulties of race relations and integration and have always tried to play a positive role in helping the process along realising that the essential requirement is in co-operation.

An opportunity to put across my thinking came in an address I was invited to deliver at the Manchester Agency for Economic Development in May 1985, an extract of which follows:

"Immigrants of whatever creed or colour coming into a new society, are always faced with a number of handicaps, some real or perceived. It may be language, the level of certain skills, conforming to, or the adaptation of local norms and behavioural patterns, all of which may act in some way or other as the basis of prejudice of one kind or another.

Prejudice because of colour is more pronounced, and affects the individual in two ways, acceptance by what I call a kindly contemptuous tolerance, or the more extreme, abusive rejection.

The Dyke & Dryden range of ethnic toiletries and cosmetics. Inset, hair by Curly Perm

BLACK IS BEAUTIFUL FOR YOUR BUSINESS

AFRO hair products and cosmetics are a neglected market in Britain. Chemists are missing the opportunity to gain a lion's share of this estimated £10 million market, which is expected to double in size during the next five years, according to Tony Wade, Marketing Director of Dyke & Dryden Ltd the largest company specialising in the marketing and distribution of such products in Europe.

Wade says: "It is difficult to understand a situation in which many of the High Street chemists in certain areas, whilst acknowledging that Black shoppers account for between 10 and 20 per cent of their total store traffic, command no more than 2½ to three per cent of Black cosmetic sales. In the United States, five per cent Black store traffic is taken as the trigger for stocking Black cosmetic products. The American Health & Beauty Aids Institute reports that, in such stores, Black shoppers account for 15 per cent of health and beauty aid sales."

Wade goes on: "One has only to look to the States, where the

for analysing the market opportunity here, and it is notable that many more US stores have recently decided to advertise Black haircare and cosmetic products. In 1982, the Revco company, which carries more than 225 varieties of Black haircare and cosmetic products in 65 per cent of its 2,000 outlets, showed in its annual report that

Chemists are neglecting a £10 million market, says Tony Wade, of distributors Dyke & Dryden

these products accounted for 14 million dollars' sales, whilst toothpaste grossed 11 million dollars, Men's aftershave lotion made 11.5 million dollars, whereas baby powder and baby oils accounted for less than half the value of Black cosmetic products.

Recent research in the US,

promotion of Black cosmetics in the UK, the same buying incentive would exist, because Black hair and Black skin need sophisticated treatment to achieve and maintain a fashionable look," says Wade.

Currently, Selfridges and Boots are gradually expanding their shelf space for these products, selecting the more well-known brands. Independent retailers such as Maldip Ltd, Safedale Ltd and Wispville Ltd have also put a foot in the water. But more Black cosmetics are still sold through hairdressing salons and sole trade establishments, which means that many High Street chains could achieve a considerable increase in business

asking where they can bu
products. People tend to
chase their haircase and
products either in the neigh
hood in which they live, or
area surrounding their pla
work.

"But, in cases where the
Street chemists do not
these, Black people often
travel long distances to b
hair and beauty products
they need. This means tha
chemists were to make
products available, they
reap enormous benefits f
market which, up to nov
grown without much help
these outlets. Once c
began to stock these pr
however, the number
tomers making repeat p
would increase and sales
of these lines could grow
40 per cent almost overn

There is a built-in
Because Black people
specially to those outlets
for their needs, stocki
ethnic cosmetics wi
increase store traffic per
also shoppers who com
purchase hair and

Modern Chemist, February 1984

I myself like thousands of immigrants have in some ways lived through and experienced some of the problems mentioned, but will tell you that I often use each difficulty to strengthen my resolve in correcting as far as possible the problems encountered.

I have over the years been connected to various organisations, whose noble objectives are to bring about a more equitable, and a more just society, by fostering good and harmonious relations and have always contended, that here in Britain we have the best opportunity of holding up a model to the rest of the world.

Our capacity for tolerance, caring and understanding, the major ingredients are unsurpassed anywhere else, qualities which we must collectively not hesitate in bringing to bear on the needs of members of our communities less fortunate than ourselves, particularly through no fault of their own."

There is certainly the emergence of a growing small Black business sector in different parts of the country. This very encouraging trend must be welcomed by all concerned, and with my own experience it gives me cause for optimism in the years to come.

This is, however, not to play down the worrying statistics about persistent prejudice and discrimination which has to be rooted out wherever it is found. The landmark indictment of institutional racism by Justice McPherson who headed the Stephen Lawrence enquiry spells that out quite clearly.

In trying to understand the difficulties faced by the average Black person, one needs only to examine carefully the prevailing climate in which the Black community is forced to compete.

For unbiased reading I would refer the reader to two Trade Union Congress press releases: "Job prospects get worse for Black and Asian workers" (2nd December 1999) and "How racism is increasingly blighting career prospects".

Britain's Ethnic Business Federation, one of the groups pursuing equal opportunity programmes, is unique in its approach about what needs to happen in this respect. It seeks out organisations who can demonstrate their equal opportunities policies in action and rewards them. Its slogan "Seen to be Working" in this regard is very appropriate.

The effort of this group is to be greatly admired and sets an example which hopefully others will follow. As one of the recipients at its award ceremony held at the Bank of England on 26th October 1999 and hosted by the Governor himself, I was invited to give a keynote address which puts across my views. An extract from the text of my address is quoted below:

"Opportunity for ethnic people to play a full and meaningful role in the business of wealth creation, will help lay sound foundations for a more just and a more equitable society.

Equal opportunity will, in the first place, engender that sense of belonging, it will advance the prospect of the community being more self supportive, removing what is often labelled as a dependency culture. We must be resolved to fight exclusion and the lack of opportunity, for unless we do so, it could so easily perpetuate poverty for generations to come.

Our diversity is a major strength and within our many communities there is an abundance of our precious people resource which we must invest in, train and prepare to play a full part in the economy.

A recent survey, conducted by Race for Opportunity, shows that by the year 2025 the largest percentage of the working population will come from immigrant stock, which underlines the urgency for tackling and ensuring that our society is thoroughly equipped and prepared to manage and take responsibility for the challenges that lie ahead in the years to come."

I would like to concede that we are without doubt making some progress, but need to quicken the pace. The courageous approach taken by new Labour in setting in motion initiatives to involve the community in the reshaping of British society is a most welcome development.

There have been three objectives in writing this book. The first was to satisfy the call by our very many friends who have repeatedly asked for it; secondly in the hope that our story may perhaps be of help to some who find themselves in the same position as we did; and thirdly to put on record our modest contribution in the struggle for equal opportunity.

Introduction

IN writing this book, I am, as it were, walking backwards from the year 2000 to the beginning of my adventure in the wider world and hopefully in the process will recapture and share with others some successes, failures, the agony with the banking institutions and how they failed the UK's Black business community.

The year 2000 saw the fulfilment of a major personal ambition, which was to winter in the sunshine of the Caribbean while retaining a pad in the UK where I had spent the best part of my adult life and indeed a part of the world that I have grown to love immensely.

Winding down from some of the organisations of which I have been a part has been quite a wrench, particularly those to do with regeneration, equal opportunity and the advancement of the ethnic community.

This was a cause I believed in and perhaps captured the essence of my belief in a speech I delivered as chairman of the Caribbean Chamber of Commerce at our 5th annual dinner at the Café Royal on 30 January 1982, which is quoted below.

"History is a story of past changes, parts of which are more important than others, not because they were longer or shorter, but because they more profoundly affect the lives of people since that time. I believe the Caribbean Chamber of Commerce is on the threshold of such a change in its history.

The spirit of self-initiative, enterprise and risk-taking is characteristic of West Indians, indeed it is this very spirit and attitude to work which brought most of us to Britain. We genuinely believed that if we worked hard and competed, that economic success would be assured, without realising that hard work and competing alone were not enough for community success.

We could only measure our success in terms of our stake in the means of production, distribution, and the service industries by sharing and owning in the economic life of Britain, nothing less would satisfy. We know we live in difficult times, and you may well ask, what is it that motivates; that propels some of us to press on at a time when the odds are stacked against our businesses, facing innumerable difficulties of one kind or another.

Part of the answer is nothing other than the firm conviction, the stark realisation that we form part of an industrial and commercial society and must function as such, that we must contribute and change where necessary; the realisation that unless we do it for ourselves and for our children that no one will do it for us.

It is my belief, that our whole socio-political status as a community could well depend on our ability to sustain and maintain our basic interests.

We cannot hope to improve our lot by sitting on the fence, on the fringe of society, remote as it were, from all that is happening around us. We must, out of necessity, make our presence felt, and the importance for a sound and strong economic base cannot be underrated. This is what our chamber is all about.

Some of us have taken on the role of pioneers in areas that present real challenges - in manufacturing, distribution, retailing and some service industries - and I urge you, in the face of these challenges, to let us hold before us our objective, our sense of purpose, and assert that the community will to succeed, in so doing our chamber will have played its part."

The response to the speech was positive and produced a standing ovation as if the entire audience was of the same mind. I was overwhelmed by the comments expressed later.

Sid Burke, the radio journalist and producer of the Sunday programme "Rice & Peas", carried the full text of the speech the following day, thus widening the chamber's audience and winning wide spread support for its work.

Among the distinguished guests that evening was Sir John Wheeler, Home Office Minister with special responsibility for ethnic minorities, and he duly gave the nod to expect government support for our work.

Returning to my winding down, June saw the end of my formal

contractual arrangements with Dyke & Dryden Ltd after 32 years. The company which has been intricately interwoven into part of my life and, quite coincidentally, ushered in what was to be one of the most deeply moving and rewarding career moments of my life. It came as a totally pleasant surprise, in the form of a letter [see facing page] which signalled what was to come.

The moment of truth arrived, and as it happened both Len and Dudley were both unable to attend leaving me alone to face what could truly be described as being spectacularly awesome.

There were, for me, moments of embarrassment as faces popped up at every turn calling me by name, faces to which I could not put names, some of whom by then would interject with what turned out to become a familiar phrase, "don't you remember".

In any event, the choice of venue, the Marcus Garvey Library in Tottenham, was intriguing, and whether it was chosen by design was not for me to question. Suffice to say, it could not have been more appropriate for, as it happens, Marcus Garvey, for my colleagues and I, had always been an inspirational hero. Another good reason, too, was that the company was founded and traded in Tottenham from where it built its national and international linkages and reputation.

Host, Juliet Alexander, who I knew well, comes from a media background. She had done her homework well in setting the scene for some great entertainment as artist after artist poured their souls out in verse, song, music and story telling, punctuated with great humour by the well respected Ralph Straker from the Toast Masters Club.

The committee had obviously invested much time and effort in their planning, organising something wonderfully special, with every act acknowledged with thunderous applause, leaving me lost for words in saying thank you to our community for the honour they have bestowed on us. We accept this mark of respect with great humility, and for me this event will live forever in my memory. For my part, I will remind ourselves of the words of the great Marcus Garvey, "Now we have started to speak, and I am only the forerunner of an awakened Africa that shall never go back to sleep".

There has been much guessing about the history of Dyke and Dryden Ltd, in particular because of the widely held view that Black people are innately mistrustful of each other in business and

Karia Press
(Tributes)
c/o Buzz Johnson
6 Ladybower Court
Gilpin Road, Clapton
London E5 0HJ
020 (8) 986-4143

5 June, 2000

Mr Tony Wade
108 Clive Road
Enfield EN1 1RF
Middlesex

Dear Mr Wade,

Re: Evening in Tribute to "Dyke and Dryden" (*Dudley Dryden, Len Dyke and Tony Wade*)

Following my recent telephone conversation to you about the above, I am writing to give you further information.

We are very keen to have yourself, Mr. Dyke and Mr. Dryden (health permitting) in attendance at this unique community tribute.

The background to the event is that we feel that our community should have the opportunity to honour our pioneers, personalities and activists during their lifetime and to provide inspiration for other generations.

The evening will focus on the contributions made by the company and its directors both in spearheading a successful business venture during harsh times and against the tide, and in nurturing other businesses and cultural activities.

We anticipate an evening of celebration which will be both nostalgic and inspiring to present and-up-and-coming Black business persons and other members of the community.
It will be hosted by Journalist Juliet Alexander, and will take place at:
The Marcus Garvey Library
Tottenham Leisure Centre
1 Philip Lane
London N15

On Friday 30 June, 2000
From 7:00 to 10:45 pm.
Please confirm your attendance.

We will also be grateful for the following, for both publicity and a display:

- Photographs (these will be returned)
- Short biographies of the directors
- A short business history

Please let us have details of relatives, friends, associates, and colleagues that you wish to be present.

Looking forward to hearing from you.

Yours sincerely

Buzz Johnson
Director **Karia Press**

that failures are in the main down to this mistrust.

This is a fallacy, and the Black community must be careful when subscribing to these opinions. The views are baseless and without foundation, and have the profoundly negative effect of destroying enterprise initiatives within the community.

Dyke & Dryden is a case in point and could so easily have fallen victim to this negative way of thinking. As it happens, there were six partners involved in the formation of the business but at the last moment, when there was the call for money on the table, four dropped out over the unfortunate issue of mistrust. This left Len Dyke and Dudley Dryden to face the music by themselves. I came on board later, more about which will follow.

From this near miss start, the company's achievements were to become an integral part, inextricably inter-woven into the historic business fabric of Black community enterprise in the UK.

Highly successful, extremely productive, commercially and socially enlightened is the mirror image through which the company has been seen in the eyes of the Black community and the public at large.

The way we were seen accords very much with the aspirations of our community, and company policy, right from the start, included a measure of ethical and compassionate conscience, balanced with realism, and demonstrated by the company's day-to-day activities. We strongly believed that social responsibility and profits need not be mutually exclusive and I will show later how our convictions have worked for our community.

The roots of the company are to be found in the music industry. The lingering sweet sounds of ska, blue beat, calypso, reggae and soul - favourites of fun-loving West Indians - were imported and sold by the company, making it possible for music from 'home' to brighten up the long, cold and dark days of winter from what became known as the people's store in West Green Road, north London.

Music as a launch pad was a unique entry point into the market place. The products sold were not available in the general music stores in the high street, especially 'pre-release' records produced in Jamaica without labels. These records fed the appetite of the many sound systems which provided entertainment for dances and the many house parties which were the order of the day.

...sion in London. Mr. ... and his wife were in town recently on a brief visit.

Praises for Dyke & Dryden

By George Ruddock

Dyke and Dryden Ltd., one of Britain's most successful black hair product distributors, continued its 25th anniversary celebration with a reception and dinner at the West Indian Cultural Centre, Clarendon Road, North London on September 23.

Heading the guest list were the Mayors of two London boroughs, Cllr Mary Nuener of Haringey and Cllr Shuja Shaikh of Hackney. Other guest speakers were Mr. Claude Brooks, Chair of the West Indian Standing Conference, and Mr Edward Brydson, Chair of the West Indian Leadership Council (Haringey).

In his welcoming address, Mr. Lincoln Dyke, founding director of the firm, spoke of the early days in getting the business started and the task to keep it going. He urged other West Indians, especially the younger generation, to get into business as this was the way forward for the community.

Cllr Mary Nuener brought greetings from Haringey and congratulated the company on reaching such an important milestone. Both men, she said, established the business because they recognised the needs of the ethnic community in establishing their own identity. She wished them continued success.

Cllr Shaikh spoke of the strong community links which Dyke and Dryden Ltd. has managed to maintain over the years. He reiterated the call for young people to take up the challenge and continue the work started by both men.

Mr Brooks recalled his early association with both Mr Dyke and Mr Dryden, especially during the formative years of the West Indian Standing Conference, while Mr Brydson praised the company for its service to the community.

Mr Dryden, in his usual inimitable style, gave a colourful history of the company, but warned his audience of the need for unity within the community in preparation for changes in 1992 when Europe opens its doors.

Planned

The vote of thanks to the many hairdressers and salons associated with the company over the years, and the dedication of the staff at Dyke and Dryden was given by Mr Tony Wade, director.

This function follows the company's 25th Anniversary dinner at the Inn on the Park in June. Other anniversary receptions are planned for South London and Birmingham later this year.

The Weekly Gleaner, October 1990

NOT a hair out of place for this proud party. Messrs Dudley Dryden, Len Dyke and Tony Wade (standing at back left to right) celebrate the 25th anniversary of their hair-care firm, Dyke and Dryden, in the presence of Haringey Mayor Mary Neuner andHackney Mayor Shuja Shaikh at the Westindian Cultural Centre recently

Caribbean Times, October 1990
(courtesy of Hansib Publications)

Dyke & Dryden became famous for the latest 'pre-release' labels, building an impressive customer base from which to offer additional services. Soon, thereafter, hair preparations and cosmetics were added to the stock lines carried, which represented a major turning point.

Len, Dudley and I belonged to the same community groups, and during a conversation after one of our group meetings, I told them about a business project on which I had embarked. They both offered their congratulations, wished me well, but later wondered if I would care to join them in their enterprise. They explained that I should give careful consideration to their offer, remarking that the going was tough, and that they would welcome some investment, but more importantly some managerial assistance. I said that I would sleep on it and come back with an answer in due course.

My limited managerial experience was derived from my position as credit controller and bank reconciliation clerk at the Smart Weston Group of companies at their head office at Eden Grove in north London. I was bitten by the business bug and motivated, in part, by my former boss, Louis Segal, the finance director for the group.

While working for Smart Weston, I developed and coined what has been referred to as the "CS Purchasing System". Simply put, the system seeks to show buyers and businesses in overseas markets ways in which they can improve their bottom line. The system was duly put to the test by way of a mail shot which produced excellent results, the first coming in from the Bahamas.

To change course at this juncture was in a way the biggest decision I had to make at the time. The answer is now history, and here I am writing it. It is well worth noting that my colleagues insisted on a name change to Dyke, Dryden & Wade which I felt was wholly unnecessary.

With all the legal instruments in place, I acquired one third of the equity in the business and started my new career as director and company secretary on 12 June 1968. The journey has been an education, one full of challenges, obstacles and frustrations, but equally fulfilling and rewarding.

The building of an industry usually takes at least a generation, and in each generation there are always pioneers. Len Dyke, Dudley Dryden and I are privileged to belong to this select group. We did not realise that we were making history in those formative years, since we were

Dyke & Dryden's Twentieth Birthd

Caribbean Times, October 1985 (courtesy of Hansib Publications)

BLACK BUSINESS

A special meeting was held last week at the Haringey Civic Centre, where the development of black business was under discussion.

Representatives from the GLC, the TUC, the Co-op Bank and Haringey's Black Business Project attended the meeting, covering subjects such as proposals for business projects, and the training of young blacks to enter the business world.

Our picture shows John Rogers of the Trades Union Council; Tony Wade of the Caribbean Chamber of Commerce; and Colin Rigg of the Manpower Services Commission.

Haringey Advertiser, July 1983

preoccupied with ensuring that our products and services met customer demands. In short, there was always too much work to be done.

Britain's Black hair care industry is today the single most important industry in which the Black community has a stake, and one which provides thousands of jobs and a small measure of economic independence created by the community itself.

Once getting on board, the most pressing and immediate requirement was to review where we were, and prepare an appropriate business plan setting out our goals and objectives and how we would achieve them given our scant cash resources.

An internal stock audit and analysis quickly pointed to major weaknesses in stock purchases, rotation, and resource allocation. We were grossly over stocked on records and short on cosmetics, hair preparations and wigs which produced the highest margins. A top priority was to address this situation as quickly as possible.

Having identified the problem, the next step was to convince my colleagues that we must change direction. This entailed some soul searching which was understandable having made their name in the record industry.

The facts and figures, however, spoke for themselves. Badly needed cash was stocked on the shelves, covered in dust and strangling the business. My findings were accepted and my recommendations were agreed, and a new era in our history had begun.

An immediate 'fire sale' of our record stocks was organised, leaving many of our loyal customers baffled at the news that we were getting out of the music business. This news, however, received a positive response from a beauty-conscious and product-starved female population.

The retailing side of the business

OUR first serious attempt in meeting established local demand was in retailing from our store at 43 West Green Road, already widely known for its records.

The store was soon to become internationally known for the widest selection of ethnic hair care and cosmetics available in the UK attracting customers from near and far.

What was to follow laid the foundation of the ethnic hair care industry and changed for all times the plight of Black people's impoverished choice of suitable hair and skin care preparations.

Entering the industry at the retail end was for me a stroke of good fortune. I was soon to learn that the shop floor was the place where you learn and gain a broad picture of the market place.

It is the place to meet the public, who will tell you what their needs are, and from there on its up to the entrepreneur to make every attempt to satisfy those needs, building happy customer relations and in the process, the business.

The shop floor is the place for information gathering, for product testing, for sampling and feedback, for getting to know your customers, earning their respect and, in fact, the front line where the real action is, for information gathering on which business decisions are made.

My career in the industry started on the shop floor and progressed through the many different segments of it - buying, sales and marketing, wholesaling, distribution, manufacturing - and gaining along the way practical hands-on management of the business and a rounded understanding of the industry as a whole.

It is often said that necessity is the mother of invention, and quite frankly this has been my experience, coping with the many areas of responsibility that landed on my lap.

Demand at West Green Road grew to such an extent that a second location was needed to serve the market. One was found in the busy Ridley Road Market in Hackney, where the infamous racist Oswald Mosley conducted his rallies against the Jewish community.

Acquiring the lease on 40 Ridley Road was like being put through an obstacle course. It took the good offices of a great Jewish friend, Harry Lester, to front the purchase of the lease for us, so extreme was racial discrimination at the time.

This was a remarkable and noteworthy deed, one for which we have been eternally grateful. Harry also owned the adjoining leases, and on his retirement sold them to us.

The additional space was timely, for it provided us with significantly better display, the ability to carry much larger stocks thus beefing-up our overall trading position. Our customers loved it, for it was, as it were, for them - one-stop shopping, finding so much of their foods and beauty needs in one location.

Although Ridley Road was a busy and bustling market place and good for our business, it was in a way a very lonely place. For years we were the only Black-owned business in a market that traded millions of pounds in produce consumed by the Black community.

The absence was not for the want of trying to obtain shops or market stalls, but primarily because of the discrimination by the landlords who owned the shops or the council inspectors who issued the street trading licences.

In any test of tolerance in those early days there is little doubt that we would have come out on top of the class for the daily diet of insults and abuse which we had to endure. Damage to our property was a regular occurrence, much of which was designed to try and drive us out of the market. Fortunately, the sturdy stuff of which we were made proved too much for them to handle.

In the meantime, an attack from another quarter came as a massive bombshell. Some months after the purchase of the two additional leases from our good friend Mr Lester, a letter arrived from British Rail requiring the site of our three shops for a proposed railway station.

Why us, we asked? We had been through so much and now big brother had stepped in to boot us out of a parade of over a hundred shops. This seemed, on the face of it, to have all the makings of some kind of Machiavellian plot, considering all the things that had gone before.

generous and proud.

Many of these people, I surmised, would be customers of Tony Wade and his burgeoning cosmetics business, Dyke & Dryden of north London. Wade describes himself as being in 'the confidence building' industry. The success of Dyke Dryden (of which he is the chairman) not only reflects an increasing disposable income among blacks, but an increasing optimism.

'You do not beautify yourself just to stand in the dole queue. We are helping people prepare for success.'

With his Jaguar and his prospering business, his active participation in church and community, Wade surely represented the emerging black middle class.

He did not disagree. He spoke of America, which he had visited often (his wife is American). There the movement of black

THE NEW MIDDLE CLASS

Though black people are frequently depicted as a 'problem' in this country, the reality is that many of them are businessmen, teachers, academics and professionals. Mick Brown identifies a silent but growing majority

Woman's Journal, October 1986

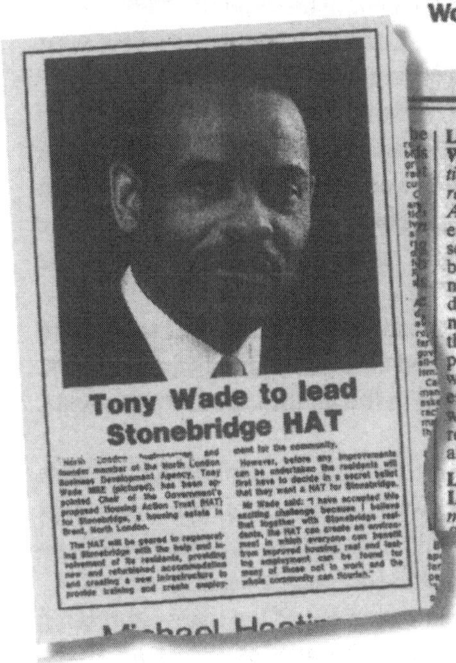
Tony Wade to lead Stonebridge HAT

LONDON — TONY WADE, *Public Relations Officer Montserrat Overseas Peoples Alliance:* The existence of the CRE sounds good in theory but in practice it has made little or no difference to the ethnic communities in this country. It is important that we should still keep talking with the view of convincing the establishment that the problem is really with the host community; the fact is they refuse to accept people. The ball has always been in their court."

LONDON — WILLIAM TRANT, *Chairman Westindian*

Westindian Digest, June 1980 (courtesy of Hansib Publications)

The Weekly Gleaner, February 1994

We questioned the logic of this and could get no reasoned answer, and could not help concluding that this smelled like institutional racism. We decided to fight it, well aware that it was like David taking on Goliath.

Our advisors could see no grounds for wanting our particular site, and with the support of our many friends we rejected British Rail's demand outright and marshalled support for our position.

The local Market Traders Association was approached for their support which they agreed in principle. However, when it came to active support by way of signatures and petitions, attending meetings and campaigning, we were left on our own.

Fortunately, our customers were marvellous, providing thousands of petitions for presenting to Hackney Council who would have to give planning permission for the new station.

As luck would have it, Dudley Dryden was vice chairman of Hackney Race Relations Council, and did some fine community work in many areas in the borough. He succeeded in getting the support of Councillor Bob Blackman, the then leader of the Council, who supported our view and suggested a different site should be found.

In the meantime, British Rail were still determined to kick us out of the market and offered us premises outside the market which, in our opinion, was unsatisfactory. After due consideration, we rejected their offer. The matter then proceeded to tribunal, where the Council rejected planning permission and with solid support across the borough we eventually won the day.

The ugly face of racism reared its head again when in 1982 we decided to open a store in the up-market Wood Green Shopping City complex. We made three applications, meeting in full all the stated requirements, but failed even to get a response.

Vacancies were still being advertised and we applied for a fourth time, this time through our solicitors who cited discrimination. A prompt response with a listing of the available units was duly received from which we selected one that became the company's flagship store.

These episodes are merely some examples of the many stumbling blocks which are unnecessarily put in the way of emerging Black businesses.

Off-loading part of my work load was an absolute necessity if we

PROFILE: Speaking to one of Britain's leading entreprene

Tony Wade MBE

The country doesn't owe you anything, nobody owes you. If you've got to do something then you've got to do it for yourself

"I would say that the first thing one would need, having decided on what you want to do, is that you have to have a dogged determination. Having set your goal, then you've got to keep at it and work hard.

"I always take the view that the world doesn't owe anybody a living, anything that one achieves you owe to yourself. That, in fact, has been my approach to life all along.

"My success is very relevant, I don't want to fly in the face of heaven and discount what one has achieved, but it *is* very relevant. I think the most satisfying thing, as far as I'm concerned, is that I've been able to provide work for myself and for quite a number of people. And this does give me some satisfaction. You could perhaps take it even further and say there's satisfaction in making a contribution and *that* is what I would call successful, *not* the material side of things.

"The company (Dyke & Dryden) has a very broad based (employment) policy. We do make a special emphasis of ensuring that we bring on board young talent. This is important for many reasons. Understanding the situation that us immigrants were finding ourselves in we have a responsibility not only to ourselves but to our children and our children's children, and as I said earlier on, the country doesn't owe you anything, nobody owes you, if you've got to do something, you've got to do it for yourself.

"Having said that, providing an opportunity for young black people has been one of the sights that we have set ourselves and it's very nice to see that we have succeeded. I look around today and there are many people now who have gone out into the wider market as managers, accountants, sales people, typists and personnel who have come through here and have had their training through *here* – now that gives me an immense source of satisfaction.

"We are an equal opportunities employer and practise no discrimination *whatsoever*, this is another goal that we have set for ourselves and this again arose out of the main from all the sufferings that we have had.

"You could look today and you would notice that as you go around our offices and stores you will find a lot of

white people, Asia
and black people fro
over the world and
course is very deli
believe that what
done at Dyke &
we're setting a
large companie
long time have
doing what reall
done and that is
example the stan
should be followe

"To get the bes
education is extren
tant, but I rememb
thing that I read m
ago that 'knowledg
the way but failure
right will leave the
and confused'.

"As people beco
ched in the system
the behavioural pat
comes part of it, it
mean abandoning y
ture. Children who
here, young black Br
you wouldn't or you
expect them to be an
other than young, Bri
black and proud of it.

"You live here and
entitled to the best of
thing. If you don't do
how are you going to
of the community? You
live in the best places,
must share the best edu
tion, you must go throu
the school system and
come governors, lawye
bank managers and eve
thing, and of course, it
of the whole process.

"Don't forget, whic
think a lot of our peo
forget, nobody's goin
it on a plate for you.
why I've got to say y
to achieve and you'
earn it. If you don't
hell then who's goin
for you. You've got
for yourself. If you'v
cided something you
do, go for it, attack it,
all that you've got and
can do that then you'll
niche and your place in
ty."

Root, May 1988 (courtesy of Hansib Publications)

were to progress. The first area of responsibility I needed to relieve myself of, was the day-to-day management of our stores which passed to a very able member of staff, Mrs Elsa Robinson, a hairdresser by profession, and our first employee in this department.

Control of the main source of weekly cash that fuelled the growth of the business could not be taken lightly and Elsa brought to the table all the ingredients that made the business fly. Her all-round skills and dedication to the company were exemplary.

Under her brilliant management and watchful eye, the retail division prospered. As a hairdresser she was able to handle all the very many technical questions about hair loss, breakage or dealing with the ongoing obsession of what to use to make the hair grow, or what were the merits of one product against another.

In those early days it was like managing a surgery, and you were expected to have answers to all the customers' questions. One question that always stood out came from white mothers of mixed-race children, or those with adopted Black children. "I am at a loss as to what to do with my child's hair, please can you help?"

Cases like these are always both sensitive and touching, and staff were trained in how to handle them. Children with short hair presented little or no problem whatsoever, as products with a high glycerine content would always loosen tight curly hair, making it soft and manageable. On the other hand, long hair may have to be cut, or treated with a specially formulated relaxer for children.

Elsa was a gifted communicator in imparting knowledge, and among her many roles, was the induction of all new sales personnel for the stores, and delivery of our ongoing educational training programme.

Wigs and hair attachments are high fashion accessories, and it was always a delight listening to her spinning a great selling line. "Smart women's wardrobes," she insisted, "should never be without a collection of the fashions of the day."

She would also explain that for a busy woman, wigs were also a welcome necessity especially where there were countless demands on her time with none to spare for the hairdresser. Wigs, she assured the customer, were the answer.

Despite the road blocks of Ridley Road and Wood Green, it would be true to say that we were filled with a sense of purpose, and nothing was

BLACK BUSINESS CONFERENCE

Mr. A.E.S. Wade, Chairman of the UK Caribbean Chamber of Commerce.

EARLIER this year, the first national Black Business Promotion Conference was held in London. Jointly sponsored by the UK Caribbean Chamber of Commerce (UKCCC) and the Commission for Racial Equality, it was extremely well-attended, by black businessmen and women. Speakers included Thernam McKenzie, Executive Vice President of M & M Products Company, USA, Carl O. Whittaker, Chairman of the Black Community Council, Quebec, Canada, and the Rt. Hon. Michael Heseltine, MP Secretary of State, Department of the Environment.

Also present were Councillor Sam Springer, the black Mayor of Hackney, John MacGregor, MP and Sir George Young, MP, with representatives from West Indian and African High Commissions, the major clearing banks, the New Nigeria Bank, the Co-operative Bank and the Trustee Savings Bank, plus representatives from the Confederation of British Industries, the Manpower Services Commission, and the Trades Union Congress.

The Conference opened with speeches by Mr. A.E.S. Wade, Chairman of the UK Caribbean Chamber of Commerce, and Mr. Peter Tucker, Chief Executive of the Commission for Racial Equality. In his welcoming address, Mr. Wade said to the bankers, "Your presence is

CHANGING ATTITIDE

First to speak was John MacGregor, MP, Under Secretary of State, Department of the Environment, and the Minister responsible for small businesses in the Government. Regarding the hindering of finance to small businesses, he said, "So often, the problem is that people don't know how to put their proposition to the bank. This applies particularly to the Caribbean Community. However, I do think that there is now a changing attitude in the bankers." He continued, "I believe that there is a tremendous opportunity in this country, and what I want to see happen here is much more of that 'spirit of enterprise' emerging from the Westindian community, because success breeds on success, and the more we can talk about success stories, the more we can overcome the disadvantages I know you suffer from."

"The two biggest problems are Finance and Advisory Services." However he stressed," I take the view that, schemes such as financial assistance, financial guarantees and so on, purely for any particular minority group of any

John MacGrefor, MP who sa want schemes purely for a minority group."

scheme, which is available businesses, and which is encourage additional lendi businesses in circumstanc they would not otherwise through existing means. W want to see is a bigger tak loan guarantee scheme Caribbean community, beca it is a scheme that would of you."

UNEMPLOYMENT

David Lee, Assistant Genera of the Trades Union Congr a changing attitude by th He remarked, ". . . th community must be able to risky opportunities, for

Black Affair, September 1982

going to stop us from pressing on, or deflect us from the goals we had set ourselves. Another five stores were subsequently opened in other London locations, together with a unit in Birmingham that doubled as retail and wholesale.

The retail sector of the business had now grown to eight stores which called for focused attention with divisional status. In addition to the specialist items carried, our customers and the public in general required all the associated toiletries such as tooth paste, deodorants and the like.

Responsibility for building this product category of the business fell on the shoulders of Dudley Dryden and his team which turned out to be superbly complementary and productive. The experiment of crossing over into the general market cosmetic sector, neatly got rid of a negative which existed for sometime, much to our disadvantage. White customers who wanted to support us, complained that there was nothing for them in our stores, overlooking one important fact, that our route into toiletries was via an unfulfilled niche left by the general market.

Catering for the general market after our initial experiment, became standard company policy within limits of affordability without being to the detriment of our core business. This policy was extended to all our outlets.

The retail outlets also served as locations for paying for or collecting airline tickets to the Caribbean which were purchased through our travel business, Dyke & Dryden Travel, and the Inter-Caribbean Social Club, which handled our charter flights operations from time to time.

Quite apart from the employment opportunities the stores provided, they acted as meeting places for countless organisations who were engaged in community matters of mutual interest. These sometimes included social events, cultural expositions, supplementary school programmes, and issues to do with Black youth and the police, a subject in which Dudley Dryden was heavily engaged.

Service to the community was in many ways the company's hallmark, and thousands of loyal customers showed their appreciation by supporting its other commercial activities.

One community activity that stood out which was of mutual benefit, was the annual "Miss Dyke & Dryden" beauty pageant and ball held annually for many years. These glittering social events, held at various quality hotels, provided a welcome respite from the drudgery of everyday

Distributor News

Anthony Wade–Developing Business in the U.K.

"Our marketplace is the world; and nothing shall deter us from reaching and maintaining that goal," says Anthony Wade, managing director and co-owner of Dyke and Dryden Ltd., center of a developing multi-million dollar international Black cosmetics industry in the United Kingdom.

A major distributor of Black hair and skin products in Britain, Dyke and Dryden is currently celebrating its 25th year of successful Black entrepreneurship. The company was founded in 1965 after Jamaican natives Lincoln Dyke and Dudley Dryden recognized a clear need for Black hair care products in Britain. Wade joined the company in 1968.

Dyke and Dryden distributes nearly all major Black hair care products in the United Kingdom. Sales representatives reach their clients either through direct contact or telesales. The company also has a cash and carry wholesale operation in both London and Birmingham, and a company-owned trucking service ensures quick deliveries.

Most importantly, however, Dyke and Dryden, and Anthony Wade in particular, is a prime example of how Black businesses are developing in the U.K., and how private agencies and the British government—through its Department of Trade and Industry and Department of Employment—are assisting in that development.

Britain experienced an influx of Black African, Caribbean, East Indian and Pakistani immigrants in the 1950s and '60s. Many of these new arrivals

unrest, such as the Brixton riots in 1986.

"The British government conducted an investigation into the cause of the riots," Wade says. "It soon became very evident that the reason for the riot was the lack of opportunity for sharing in the economic life of the nation. The results of the investigation indicated a number of remedies, most specifically that steps should be taken by government, local authorities and industry at large to open up opportunities to young ethnics."

Wade currently chairs the North London Business Development Agency Limited, one of five agencies initiated by the British government to improve economic conditions for Britain's growing ethnic population.

"There is also quite a bit of support from the private sector," Wade continues. "Some of that support has come in cash and some in time. For instance, we have in the U.K. what we call the Big Four: the National Westminster Bank, Barclays Bank PLC, Lloyds of London and the Midland Bank. Barclays, the second largest bank in Britain, sent one of their managers as a financial consultant to my agency. It was a learning experience for him as well. He learned first-hand what it is like for an ambitious Black to go into a bank with high hopes and come out dismayed."

"We have contributed to the development of our people in the U.K."

Wade points out that the relationship between Black/ethnic business devel-

ful, they ha
ing big, nev
In conc
governmen
essentially t
keep track
have assist
advice and
sary; to assi
for busine
sions, and
career trai
through ec
networking
"We pre
start-ups) w
Wade says.
also able to
sonable cas
our sources.
Those fin
include th
Enterprise (
up to 5,000
Princes You
designed
entreprene
and A Char
as much as
available in
"The inte
if people do
get their bus
go away hap
spoken to; th
and not just s
comments.
Wade adds
which recen
Sheen Prod
more direct r
advancemen
through emp
after a few y
contributed t

Shoptalk, September 1990

routine. They also opened a window of opportunity for girls who wished to pursue a career in modelling.

In addition to promoting the event, the company as part of its commitment to community development, quite often kitted out several of the contestants and met their related expenses enabling them to participate.

On the other hand, these events were for the company, priceless marketing opportunities in branding and product exposure, which significantly did much in building its reputation.

Outreach work with a number of organisations was common place. Barnardo's, for example, had difficulty in coping with some of their children's hair. Our work shop teams were sent in and painlessly put the mothers and children comfortably at ease. The women's prison at Holloway, the Afro Educational Project and NCH Action for Children, were all beneficiaries of our outreach efforts.

Significant cash support to a number of organisations included the National Federation of the Blind, the Metropolitan Police (Traffic) Division, the West Indian Standing Conference, The North London Business Development Agency and the UK Caribbean Chamber of Commerce. Contributions to these bodies perhaps reflect, in some small way, our belief in being an inclusive society.

Development of wholesale distribution

WEST Green Road, where the business began, remained for a time the company's administrative offices and improvised warehouse. A converted old shed at the back of the building together with the ground floor was used for storage.

Mixed container loads of stock imported from the United States was more than our retail stores could handle and it was, therefore, necessary to break the bulk by selling off the excess stock to release cash and reduce the pressure on precious space. This exercise was spectacularly successful and led directly to the development of the wholesale division.

The initial operation actually began from the boot of my car. Armed with a box of samples, price lists and an order book, I motored around to the local chemists, food and drug stores, looking for shelf space and offering new opportunities for them to increase the lines carried with a guarantee they would improve their sales. There was little need for a bullish sales pitch, for entry was far easier than I anticipated as most stores visited were already being asked for the products. Stores where some resistance was found, I offered to leave the merchandise on a sale or return basis as an introductory gesture, explaining that if the goods did not sell I would return and collect them. This arrangement suited both parties.

This introduction worked brilliantly, and everything left was sold quickly with repeat orders flooding in. With no staff in place for this initial testing exercise, all orders were personally packed by myself during the day and invoiced by night.

Order/picking lists were taken home for invoicing at night and made ready for delivery the following day. This successful pilot now urgently required a structure and system which was quickly put in place to handle these local deliveries.

Hair dressing salons had grown in substantial numbers, representing the single largest sector of independent Black-owned businesses. Their role and influence and servicing their needs was therefore of major significance.

An organisation to set standards and provide a code of conduct to regulate the profession was necessary, and Dyke & Dryden took the lead in facilitating this development. This led to the creation of the Caribbean Afro Society of Hairdressers (CASH).

The next phase in this development was to implement a London-wide delivery service followed by a national distribution network outside the capital to cover towns with large Black populations.

At this stage our growth explosion was phenomenal and overwhelmed the current management of the company. Urgent steps were needed to cope with this surge in activity. Good professional management was desperately needed, together with adequate warehousing and management systems to keep pace with our expansion.

Our early low cost operation now needed a much more rounded corporate structure, which was to further test the founders' staying power in this new environment. Recognising this need in itself was part of the answer.

Funding this leap forward became a crisis. Up to this point we were trading for cash with a nominal bank facility of £2,500, the original borrowing at the setting up of the business. It is also appropriate to mention at this point that the above sum was secured by way of a second charge on the homes of the three partners and the life insurance we had at the time.

With the help of our auditors Newman Harris & Co., a reputable firm based at Cavendish Square in London's West End, we approached our bankers with a properly costed programme for vans, increased stock holding and additional staff.

Annual turnover at the time was £250,000 and cashflow projections showed quite clearly that the £10,000 we were looking for could easily be met. But our small borrowing request was rejected by our bank manager without a word of explanation.

This was a major blow, and explains just how some bank managers held back legitimate Black businesses with sound track records.

All the evidence in this particular case, leaves us to come to only one conclusion, that of blatant discrimination because of our colour. On the

DISTRIBUTOR PROFILES

Distributor Profiles

Photo courtesy of Anthony Wade

Anthony Wade
Managing Director
Dyke & Dryden Ltd.
19 Bernard Road
Tottenham, London N 15 4 NE
01-801-7321

Founded by Caribbean immigrants in 1965, Dyke & Dryden Ltd. is one of the most successful Black enterprises in Europe today. In 1968, Anthony Wade, formerly an accountant in the garment business, became their managing director.

During his 21 years in management, Wade is most proud of an award Dyke & Dryden received in 1984 from Prime Minister Margaret Thatcher for shipping exports from Britain to other parts of the world. A socially conscious company, Dyke & Dryden participates through business in the community to help revitalize urban development. They also lobby for the community and are a model in the area of equal opportunity employment for other companies.

To be in better touch with the consumer, Dyke & Dryden owns and operates six retail stores. Like the parent company, these stores specialize in offering all of the major hair care products. C.H.

Philosophy: "The customer is the cornerstone of our business," Wade says. "And service to the customer comes first."

Shoptalk, Summer Journal, 1989

...to the best of their abilities.

At times, however, I have been ...

and here again we must look to the institutions of learning to assist in ...

U.K. Caribbean Chamber of Commerce

"Serious Business"

The Right Honourable Mr. Errol Walton Barrow, M.P., former Prime Minister of Barbados now leader of the Opposition was in London recently and paid a visit to the Chamber where he had discussions about black business development in Britain with Mr. Collin Carter, and Mr. Tony Wade, Secretary and Chairman respectively of the Chamber. Mr. Barrow expressed keen and great interest on the subject and would be exploring ways of how people in the Caribbean at official level could be of assistance.

Left to right: Mr. Collin Carter, Secretary of the Chamber, The Right Honourable Mr. E. W. Barrow, MP, and Mr. Tony Wade, Chairman of the UKCCC.

UK Caribbean Chamber of Commerce Newsletter, June 1982

suggestion of our auditors we decided on a change of bank and succeeded in getting an offer of £15,000 from another bank based on the same forecast offered to our previous bank.

The bankability of the Black community has been discussed from time to time in a number of forums, a concept which in my opinion is contemptuous to say the least. The simple truth is that the element of risk taken by individual managers, with guide lines of discretion within the institutions, seemed not to apply to Black-owned businesses because of the perception that they are all bad risks.

This is nothing other than a mere figment of the imagination as decent managers must know. Where there is adequate lending discretion, the problem is, I believe, with the person behind the lending desk.

I came to this conclusion about a month after our request was rejected by our old bankers, which still remained my personal bankers. On visiting the branch, I noted there was a new man who seemed approachable. I made an appointment to see him, discussed a personal need I had for a £22,000 loan and came away with the loan all neatly wrapped, based on my previous history at the branch.

With new money in place, steps were immediately taken to implement our expansion programme. A recruitment drive to find people who shared our values and were willing to make a commitment was sought.

Our earliest secretarial support was provided by a wonderfully creative friend Mrs Joan Sam, a lady always bubbling with drive and enthusiasm. She was a tower of strength in those early days, bouncing ideas back and forth. Eventually, she confided to me that her true calling was to become a hairdresser and without hesitation I offered my wholehearted support and encouragement and although I would miss her, I instinctively knew that she would do well in anything she had set her mind to do. On parting I asked her to make me a small promise, that when she finished her training she would come back for a chat.

She duly returned after her training and became a key contributor in what was to become a major turning point in the company's history, more about which will follow later.

It took a while after Joan left to fill the secretarial vacancy and in the meantime, to our great surprise, a wonderful retired friend known to us only as Miss Dorman, volunteered to hold the fort until we were able to fill the post. She belonged to the old school of thoroughness and imparted

MANAGEMENT: The Growing Business

Breaking out of the ethnic boundaries

Black and Asian business people in the UK face constraints — but also growing opportunities, reports **Charles Batchelor**

Honeytop Foods turns out pittas, chapattis, tortillas and a range of other ethnic breads from its two bakeries in Hackney, East London and Leicester. While both these areas have large ethnic minority communities William Eid and his fellow directors have never seen their markets as restricted to any particular ethnic group.

"Our objective from the start was to become a supplier to the large supermarket chains because that is where the buying power is concentrated," says Eid, whose origins are Lebanese though the family lived for long time in Ghana.

The decision to go for the big supermarket chains imposed an enormous burden on the company's finances – heavy demands were put on the family savings – in its early years as it struggled to develop a range which was broad enough to meet the buyers' needs. "We had to develop a wide range of products to persuade the supermarkets to put us on their buying lists and to justify them sending a vehicle round," says Eid. It took five years before Honeytop began making a profit – in 1988.

Eid expects profits to continue to grow and with turnover of £1.8m and a staff of 35 Honeytop is now one of the leading companies in its field. Eid does not believe he encountered any racial prejudice in his efforts to build the business – though his decision to keep investing in new markets ...

Tony Wade: Planning to launch into the white market in the UK

... Tony Wade, managing director of Dyke & Dryden, a supplier of Afro hair preparations and cosmetics which has been established for 25 years, recalls visiting one company to discuss placing an order for its products.

In spite of asking to see the sales manager Wade was sent to see the works foreman. The gateman explained later that black people who came to the company were usually looking for a job in the factory.

Based in Tottenham, North ...

... of ethnic businesses.

Dyke & Dryden, for example, has capitalised on the growing UK black community and the established market in the US as well as developing exports to Africa and the Caribbean. It is also, however, planning to launch into the white market in the UK.

Once a business has survived the early difficult years the problems which are specifically related to the colour of its owner diminish. "The problems we face – of finding skilled managers and finance – are the problems of any industry rather than anything related to being a black business," comments Tony Wade.

Financial Times, September 1990

some lessons which left their mark on the business. This act of kindness is a memorable one which had to be remembered in the Dyke and Dryden story.

Mrs Pearl Goodridge filled the post magnificently and later became Office Manager and then Personnel Manager. She did a great job in putting together a good administrative unit which made all the difference, and beefed-up all round office efficiency.

Her skills lent themselves particularly well to organisational issues, problem-solving, conducting interviews, and report writing which made decision-making for me much easier. She was an excellent team player, very dependable and with honesty beyond reproach.

Another great find in the early days of the business was Rudi Page. He possessed great marketing and selling skills and came on board as Sales Manager, leading and inspiring a small team, who together succeeded in opening up extensive territorial presence and brand awareness across the entire country.

Rudi was later promoted to Sales and Marketing Manager and was later to play a key role in the launch of the company's subsidiary Afro Hair & Beauty. He was someone full of drive and ambition, and today runs Statecraft Consulting Ltd, a business with a good track record.

The next key appointment was for the company's own internal full time accountant to implement and manage urgently needed systems to control the business. This position was widely advertised and produced good responses from candidates with impressive backgrounds. Included in the listing was a young, newly qualified Black accountant. The sifting process was carried out by our auditors and after much discussion presented their recommendations, with emphasis on the need for experience.

We respected their views which were valid but were also acutely aware that among the many factors holding back the community was the lack of opportunity to gain experience in areas such as the one we were offering. On that basis, we selected Kingsley Peter, the newly qualified Black accountant.

He was articulate and professional in his approach to his work and lived up to our expectations, justifying the faith we had put in him. He was a 'whiz' with figures and soon earned himself the nickname, "boy genius". He represented the company well, his advice was sound and

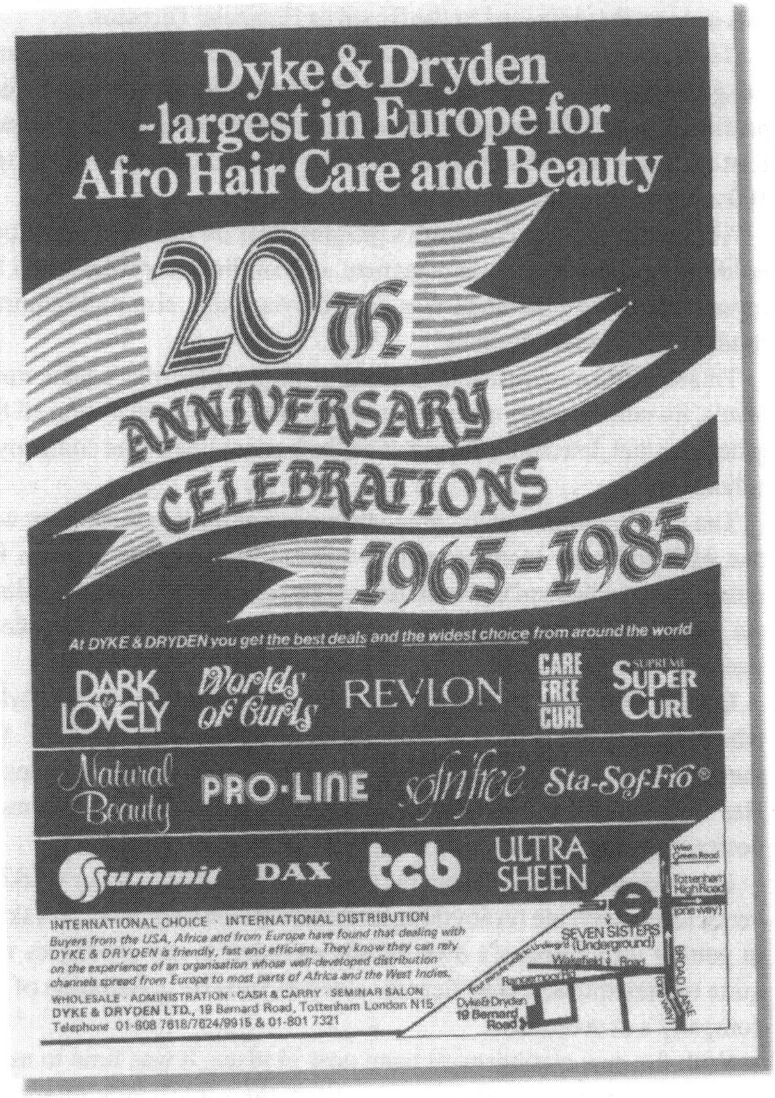

Dyke & Dryden
-largest in Europe for
Afro Hair Care and Beauty
20th
ANNIVERSARY
CELEBRATIONS
1965-1985
At DYKE & DRYDEN you get the best deals and the widest choice from around the world
DARK & LOVELY
Worlds of Curls
REVLON
CARE FREE CURL
SUPREME SUPER CURL
Natural Beauty
PRO-LINE
soft n free
Sta-Sof-Fro®
Summit
DAX
tcb
ULTRA SHEEN
INTERNATIONAL CHOICE · INTERNATIONAL DISTRIBUTION
Buyers from the USA, Africa and from Europe have found that dealing with DYKE & DRYDEN is friendly, fast and efficient. They know they can rely on the experience of an organisation whose well-developed distribution channels spread from Europe to most parts of Africa and the West Indies.
WHOLESALE · ADMINISTRATION · CASH & CARRY · SEMINAR SALON
DYKE & DRYDEN LTD., 19 Bernard Road, Tottenham London N15
Telephone 01-808 7618/7624/9915 & 01-801 7321
SEVEN SISTERS (Underground)
Tottenham High Road
(one way)
BROAD LANE
Dyke&Dryden 19 Bernard Road

Hairdressers Journal International, April 1985

was eventually promoted to the Board as Financial Director.

He has since moved on with the finest recommendation a company can give and to his great credit he has excelled to one of the most senior positions in British industry, that of Area Financial Controller, South East Network Services Division, for the National Grid, one of the top 100 companies in the country.

At the centre of the company's progress was its warehousing, stock holding and distribution management, one of the many roles filled by myself, realising that stock was key to everything else and required prudent attention at all times.

This scenario always meant evaluating the purchase of adequate stock levels, its safe keeping, its turns, and, in short, keeping an eye on all the processes that determine the result on the bottom line of the company's balance sheet.

The final appointment to complete our senior management team was that of Warehouse Manager which went to Mr Grantley Hedley. He used to be a soldier and had excellent organisational skills and discipline, the tools needed to marshal the stock pickers and packers and keep them on their toes.

On the front line of the company's efforts, was Mrs Evlyn Dyke, whom I always referred to as "the first lady of Dyke & Dryden". On the reception desk she was the first point of contact with customers. Her communication skills were brilliant and charmed the most hesitant customer.

Her performance earned her the position of Export Manager working very closely with me on anything considered to be a big deal. Her skills in getting the company's own brands included in any purchases was quite remarkable and significantly aided the market penetration of the company's own brands.

With the new management team now in place, it was time to make sure that everyone clearly understood the company's operating philosophy. We must at all times conduct our business with professionalism, honesty and integrity, raise our self esteem and the awareness of the community we serve, understanding that our success would be measured only by the service we give.

Our marketing and PR functions were handled in-house, and events which needed specialist attention were contracted out from time to time

GLC grant for Chamber

THE GLC has approved a grant application from the UK Caribbean Chamber of Commerce to establish a profesional business advisory and development service. Through this it is hoped that more positive aid will be given to members of the Chamber and the black community wanting to start their own businesses.

In a statement issued by the Chamber this week, Mr Anthony Wade, chairman, welcomed the GLC approval. "This is merely a start of a programme that is urgently needed to bring the black [illegible] munity into the eco[illegible] mainstream of [illegible] economy. The Ch[illegible] and the black com[illegible] are ready to mak[illegible] economic contrib[illegible] business, as w[illegible] already done a[illegible] earners in the pa[illegible]

It is the first [illegible] Chamber has [illegible] any kind of gr[illegible] now it hopes [illegible] government wi[illegible]

New head of U.K. Carib. C of C

ANTHONY WADE

Jamaican new Vice-President

ANTHONY WADE, a director of Dyke and Dryden Ltd., has been elected Chairman of the U.K. Caribbean Chamber of Commerce. He has succeeded Pal Ganguli of Red Stripe beer in that position. Mr. Wade is one of the most active and most popular members of the West Indian community in Britain.

He was born in Montserrat and has been associated with many social organisations including the Standing [illegible]

the radio programme "Rice n' Peas", became the new Vice-Chairman. He had served previously as interim Chairman pending Mr. Ganuli's election a year ago. Mr. Burke is a pioneer of West Indian photo-journalism in London.

Collin Carter, the Barbadian director of Jetload Trading, retained his position as Secretary of the Chamber. His business is based in North London and he has contributed to welfare and community affairs.

Mr. Wade, who was previously Vice-Chairm[illegible]

as the need arose. This method of operation worked well for us leaving senior managers in control of the plans while passing on the detailed work to people on the outside.

With all our senior positions filled, for a brief moment it seemed like it was time for some respite from the rigours of the daily grind, but this was extremely difficult, not because I trusted no one but more so perhaps because the 'fix' of steering the ship had taken me over by being there first in the mornings and the last to leave at nights. Privately, staff nicknamed me 'Mr Go-go-holic', but never to my face. However, Kay Osborne, Senior Vice President of M & M, one our major US suppliers, labelled me 'the man with Dyke & Dryden with the globe on his head'. I had never questioned what she meant, but believed it had something to do with us bumping into each other in world markets.

British industry was particularly slow in dealing with what was an obvious gap in the market. Manufacturers like Cheeseborough-Ponds for example were exporting their cosmetics to the Caribbean and neglecting a market in their back garden. We were re-importing their products back into the UK to fill the gap and naturally had a good chuckle at their lack of vision which worked to our advantage.

American companies were in the forefront of product development suitable for Black hair and skin types, which were to become increasingly available in our market, across Europe and Africa. Dyke & Dryden was to play an important role in this process.

A key plank in our business plan was to ensure adequate stocks at all times, which meant establishing good channels of supply out of the US where the industry was already well developed. To accomplish this part of the plan, meant making direct contact with the key players and decision-makers in the industry. An itinerary was put together covering some five states that I was to visit - New York, New Jersey, Chicago, Tennessee and Atlanta.

My welcome during all these visits was full of warmth with everyone keen on widening their markets and seeing our meetings as a new chapter in their company's fortunes. For many, it was to become a reality. Links were established and purchases made from all firms visited and a one-to-one rapport followed with senior personnel wanting to ensure their share in what was now fast becoming a global market in the ethnic hair and skin care industry.

hand. year has also had some

Dyke & Dryden.....

DYKE & DRYDEN is one of the largest, if not the largest, Westindian-owned businesses in Britain today, with an annual turnover running into millions of pounds. The company primarily deals with hair-care and cosmetic products for the black community.

In addition to its own product range of hair-care and beauty items, the company handles hundreds of other items for the community from the American hair-care and beauty market.

A great deal of Dyke & Dryden's business is done in Africa, the Caribbean and Europe. The company also has a very large slice of the black market in Britain.

Dyke & Dryden was started back in the early sixties by Len Dyke and Dudley Dryden, who were later joined by Tony Wade. Today the company is run by the three partners.

Each of the partners look after a specific area of the company's business, which extends to travel and shipping, the running of three shops in north London and a large warehousing and distribution enterprise.

Anthony Wade,

The company, like any other business, has been hit by the recent recession. However, under its three able partners it has been coping reasonably well with sitting out the recession while waiting for the upturn.

When *Caribbean Times* spoke to Tony Wade of Dyke & Dryden, he had this to say:

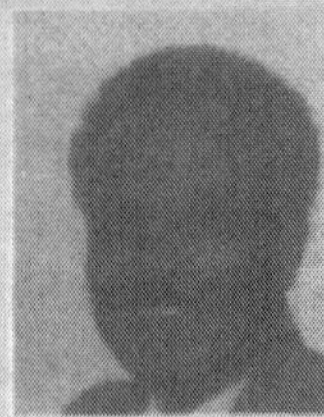

Len Dyke,

"The recession has more adversely affected the black community than any other section in the country. Naturally it has meant that our business has also been affected, but we are coping. People obviously have less money to spend, and so are less able to do the things they want to do".

Apart from the recession in Britain, Dyke & Dryden has been steadily increasing its trade with Africa and the Caribbean. It has not always been easy for Dyke & Dryden; there were times when they did not enjoy the kind of facilities they have today. Like any other fledgling black business, they initially had difficulties in securing a loan.

On this Tony Wade says, "I think there are still too many barriers put up against young black entrepreneurs, who might otherwise succeed were it not for such obstacles."

Meanwhile, Dyke & Dryden stands today as a living testimony to what can be achieved by black businesses if only they are given a fair crack of the whip. In just under 20 years they have been able to push themselves by dint of hard work and determination into the forefront of black enterprise. Truly a most remarkable success story.

Dudley Dryden

Caribbean Times, December 1984
(courtesy of Hansib Publications)

Gary Gardener, president of the US-based Soft Sheen Inc., shared with me his vision. He had explained that his sights were set on the world as his market, reasoning that in the US his market was limited to a mere thirty million people, whereas in Africa alone he could have access to in excess of two hundred million people. His vision and thinking made an impression on me and little did I know that in that first meeting he also had Dyke & Dryden as a target, in which Soft Sheen eventually bought a controlling interest in November 1987.

One of the major players in the industry at the time was Therman McKenzie, President of the giant corporation, M& M Products. During his speech at a conference in London, staged by the UK Caribbean Chamber of Commerce, of which I happened to be chairman at the time, he dubbed the UK as "the fifty-first state" as far his company was concerned. His glee was certainly understandable because in 1982, when he made this remark, purchases by Dyke & Dryden from his company were in excess $1 million dollars in that year.

The conference was a high profile affair, attended by the Rt. Hon Michael Hestletine, the then Secretary of State for the Environment, and the Minister for Small Firms, Mr John McGregor. It was aimed at drawing attention to the difficulties Black business people faced in their search for funding.

All the major UK banks were represented and the conference had as its theme, 'Ethnic business development and the role of the banks'. McKenzie's keynote speech as a self-made Black American multi-millionaire, did much in highlighting some of the steps needed to be taken by banks on this side of the Atlantic. It was, in part, a crusade pursued by the Chamber on behalf of the Britain's Black community.

A survey of the membership after the conference, showed that little or nothing had happened to improve the desperate need for funding. The outcome was a dismal disappointment for the Chamber and its members.

What was to follow after my initial American trip laid the foundations of the ethnic hair care industry in the UK and changed for all times the plight of Black women and their impoverished lack of choice. Dyke & Dryden was to play an important role in this unhappy situation.

Fuelling the pace of development in the industry, was the breakthrough in the chemistry of hair which had a liberating effect on millions of

The Voice Interview

TONY WADE

TONY WADE: Driven by a can-do spirit

Working man's hero

Tony Wade, one of the three men behind multi-million pound hair and beauty company Dyke and Dryden, lives … by a philosophy of hard work and self-help. He suggests that others s… Roger Baird went to meet him

"Nobody's going to put anything on a plate for you. You damn well have to take it or you simply won't get it. Life's about opportunities and once you have been given a chance it's up to you to take it or you only have yourself to blame"

The Voice, May 1994

women the world over. The contention that we are never satisfied with what we have could not be truer than with hair, be it Caucasian hair or Black hair.

In the Caucasian case, people with straight hair change their hair formation by the use of thioglycolic acid on rollers to make it curly, whereas natural curly hair is processed with sodium hydroxide, a chemical used to make it straight.

In the mid-Fifties, George E Johnson, of Johnson Products Company, developed the Ultra Sheen chemical straightener process for Black hair which revolutionised the industry. He made a fortune and his was the first Black company to be floated on the New York stock exchange.

The late Seventies and early Eighties saw another revolution with the reverse use of thioglycolic processing for natural curly hair which ushered in the world-beating hair fashion of 'wet look', 'dry look', 'curly look' and 'wavy look', and a whole host of other variations which made fortunes for many companies.

Hindsight is a great teacher, for while as a company we benefited enormously from our early entry into the industry, in looking back we could spot at a glance some of our many errors.

Most of our agency distribution contracts for example, were concluded by way of a hand shake rather than in tight formal contracts. Here was lack of experience on my part, for as it turned out, once the manufacturer's brands we introduced were established in the market, loyalty went out of the window. Another fatal mistake was our policy of heavy discounting to some of our sub-distributors who later became our major competition.

The market had expanded significantly and by 1986 turnover had reached the magical figure of £5 million, which at the time was quite an achievement for a Black business in the UK. Len, Dudley and myself always regarded modesty as a virtue and the credit for this performance always went to our staff who were the backbone of the business.

Our business by its very nature was organic, and some hedging in a market that was maturing called for action to safeguard our position. Our success had spawned some big fishes who were vigorously swimming after us and a structural review was once again necessary while we were still ahead of the game.

Two options were considered. One was to diversify into property which we did by buying some of the freehold properties we occupied, and the other was to try and control our destiny by manufacturing our own brands.

The overall market place needed to be looked at however, and for this exercise we hired a consultant whose brief was to look at our strengths and weaknesses and provide a road map for the next five years.

The brief with time-scales was agreed and signed by both parties with fifty percent of the fees paid in advance and the balance paid on completion of the assignment. Two weeks before we were to receive the consultant's report, I went on a short visit to one of our suppliers in the States and was invited to lunch by the Vice President of sales. To my horror, my host produced a copy of the report we ordered which was offered to them and others at a price.

Stung by the treachery of the consultant, our well laid plans were now ruined, frustrating our attempt to stay ahead of the competition. Unknown to the consultant, however, an alternative plan was on the drawing board which only needed refinement. This was put into action with immediate effect and saved us from certain catastrophe.

We were always concerned that total reliance on American products was not in our best interests, and that steps needed to be taken to have similar items manufactured here in the UK. Preparatory work had already begun in connection with registering trade marks, product formulation and locating suitable packaging contractors to do the work.

Some good fortune was on our side in that we had a home-grown professional coming out of our own stable to carry out product tests on trial runs, monitor usage results and provide educational seminars.

Dyke & Dryden owned a seventy-five percent stake in the Supreme School of Hair Design. We later sold our entire interest in the school to the twenty-five percent stakeholder, Mrs Joan Sam, my previous secretary.

The move into manufacturing

OUR bold new stride into the world of manufacturing came with the launch of Supreme Super Curl, and as the name suggests, it was a product designed to cater for the 'curly look' and represented a major breakthrough for Dyke and Dryden.

Timing was of the essence and a key factor in the brand's success lay in the fact that hair fashions were changing and, luckily for us, we were carried along on the crest of the wave!

Quite by accident, I struck up a friendship with Paul Davies, the owner of Tor Chemicals, a manufacturing chemist based in south London who was later to become my guru and great friend. I confided in Paul what I wanted to achieve and he set to work on experimenting with formulations he had not handled before.

Enter Joan Sam of Supreme Hair Design, my previous secretary and now my business partner. Joan worked closely with Paul testing and reformulating until we eventually cracked what at first seemed impossible. This was a significant breakthrough - the first gel perm formulated and developed in the UK. It was branded and trade marked under the name, Supreme Super Curl.

The research and development breakthrough was a big one for British industry in that it removed the total dependency in the UK on US-manufactured products. Paul said, "We will always be indebted to Tony Wade for his vision and drive in pushing us into this direction, which provided much rewarding work and employment for our company."

The range comprised a gel perm, neutralising solution, shampoos, conditioners and a hairdress. At the same time, John Cobb, a design consultant, was brought on board to handle our packaging and marketing requirements including press releases.

The brand performed beyond our wildest dreams and to the extent that Tor Chemicals were unable to cope with the demand. Another contract manufacturer had to be sought in an effort to satisfy our requirements and to provide insurance against difficulties with supply.

This proved to be a delicate matter to handle, and great care had to be taken not to upset the original and painstaking technical development work done with my good friend Paul. A satisfactory solution was found by leaving the professional products with Tor Chemicals. Thioglycolic acid, the active ingredient in the gel perm which breaks down the sulphur dioxide bonds of the hair thus enabling change in its natural configuration from small tight curls into the desired size and shape, always needs to be produced at the right pH balance to ensure its effectiveness, and Paul had mastered this technique.

Chemical processing of the hair by its very nature causes substantial moisture loss, which has to be replaced by daily doses of moisturising treatments making the after care for chemically treated hair essential. The net result meant large volume sales of the retail after care items.

Manufacturing turned out to be another giant step for the company and our every move was closely monitored by our competition both at home and abroad. The Americans saw us a threat and became much more active in this market. We made much of our home-grown brands and used the slogan "Made in Britain", of which we were justly proud.

DHL, a Bradford-based company, won the contract for initially supplying the retail items for Super Curl and who eventually became our largest volume supplier but not without some gentle persuasion. At our first meeting, we sensed some unease, which turned out to be the familiar unwillingness of wanting to do business with a Black company. The owners, Donald and Tony Lang, were about to send us away but gave each other the eye across the table and in their own words, "agreed to take a chance on us".

After agreeing terms, work got underway for a trial run, and to their astonishment were forced to increase their staff levels to cope with the additional work we were putting their way. Months later, a much larger factory was acquired to accommodate our business. Their operational space increased from 5,000 sq. ft to 48,000 sq. ft.

DHL's managing director, Tony Lang, is an ardent cricket lover and among his most treasured possessions was a bat bearing the signatures of the players who took part in the England versus West Indies Test Series in 1984. He showed off his precious trophy to me and half jokingly

CT: *Supporting the community*

The man from Montserrat hots up the commercial pace

Despite obstacles, men and women of Caribbean extraction have made their mark in commerce. **Denise Saul** *talks to one of the most successful and socially-conscious leaders.*

I CORNERED Tony Wade at the end of a busy day and asked him what was his driving force. He replied: "The heights of great men reached and kept, were not attained by sudden flight, but they whilst their companions slept, were toiling upwards in the night".

As managing director of Dyke and Dryden, Tony Wade MBE has pioneered the company's growth and turned it into a multi-million pound venture. Dyke and Dryden is Europe's leading importer, distributor and manufacturer of black hair care and cosmetic products. The company started life as a record distributor in the '60s, selling records at the time of high demand for roots, culture and music.

Wade changed the company's strategy when he joined Len Dyke and Dudley Dryden in June 1968. Because of the paucity of business on this scale in Britain run by the Westindian community, Dyke and Dryden set out consciously, deliberately and purposefully to be a role model. They also provided an outlet for black people with business and managerial skills, even encouraging individuals to form partnerships and set up businesses in cosmetic retailing.

"I thought that it would be a good idea if the company started to sell black hair products," he told me. "We spotted a gap in the market place where black women were not catered for and we set out to put that right".

Over the years, Dyke and Dryden has been honoured for its achievements, and its astonishing commercial success. In 1983 it became the first company to receive the Black Business Community Award and the first company to participate in a British trade mission sponsored by the government to the Caribbean. In 1984 the company was among 37 invited to a reception for entrepreneurs at 10 Downing Street.

Anthony Edward Samuel Wade was born in Montserrat, the Westindies in 1932. His earliest ambition was to work in public administration. After finishing secondary education in Montserrat, Wade left for Britain in the early '60s where he studied Economics, Accountancy and Public Administration at Tottenham Technical College in north London.

Tony Wade started as an Accounts Clerk with the Smart Weston Group of Companies. Later he became a one-third partner in Dyke and Dryden. The Tottenham business firm sells its own British manufactured range in many countries including France, the Caribbean and some African capitals.

"The company acts as an motivating force within the community. We provide business counselling, advice and work experience for many of our compatriots. We also give people the opportunity to develop all kinds of skills".

The company has been also a major supporter of the ethnic press, advertising at a time when most Westindian papers were desperately in need of revenue. They were also conscious of the need to promote and publicise their products. The ethnic media wrote extensively about their achievements.

As a businessman with a 'scientific' approach, Tony Wade also realised the crucial role of exhibitions in which his company participated not only in this country but also in Africa. Tony Wade maintains that he has no regrets over his large advertising and promotional budget, stressing the importance of getting the sales message across, no matter how small the company.

Dyke and Dryden also formed a subsidiary company called Afro Hair and Beauty Ltd. In 1983 Afro Hair and Beauty Ltd staged its first Afro Hair and Beauty Exhibition and the Grosvenor Hotel in central London. This has since turned into an annual event. Exhibitors include major American companies already in this market, as well as a few British companies anxious to reach the black consumers who spend about three to five times as much money on hair care and cosmetic

products as their white compatriots. The Afro Hair and Beauty Show is acknowledge as Europe's premier international trade and consumer-trade exhibition.

Does Tony Wade feel the government is doing enough to help small businesses, specifically manufacturers?

"Not as much as I would like to see. Much pressure needs to be put on banks and financial institutions to help develop our full potential in the economy as a whole. On our part, black people must refuse to take no for an answer".

In 1985 Tony Wade became the director of the North London Business Development Agency, a government initiative resulting from Lord Scarman's report on the Brixton riots.

I was invited by the Home Office in 1985 to lead the agency and have remained its chairman ever since. The agency has been largely successful in meeting its remit, "the development of the ethnic businesses in its catchment."

Tony Wade has set an inspiring example to the black community and his track record is hard to beat. In 1989, Wade became the director of north London, Investments Ltd. He is director of his old college, the College of North East London and non-executive director of the New River Health Authority, covering the boroughs of Haringey and Enfield. He is also director of North London Training and Enterprise Council (TEC)

In November 1993, Wade was appointed by the Department of Environment as Shadow Chair of the Housing Action Trust (HAT) which is an urban regeneration scheme for Stonebridge, a run down estate in north London with one of the worst crime records in Greater London. HAT has a budget of £100 million. While a construction programme will be an essential part of any regeneration plan for the area, Wade believes that to offer people real hope you have to build on 'the fabric of the community'. This means investing in people and creating an infrastructure which works for the benefit of the whole community.

The Montserratian born industrialist still maintains strong ties with the church. He was a former member of the British Council of Churches (OVAC). Organ music is a subject which he talks about most passionately. Handel is one of his favourite composers.

In 1987, Tony Wade was awarded of the Order of the Member of the British Empire (MBE) and won a Hansib Community Award.

Profile of Tony Wade MBE

Born: Montserrat, Westindies, Nov 1932
Educated: Cavala Hill Secondary School, Montserrat and Tottenham Technical College
Favourite colour: 'Neutral' colours
Favourite Food: Guyanese Pepperpot
Likes: Go-getters' who refuse to take no for an answer
Dislikes: People who whinge and lack creativity
Status: Married
Transport: Jaguar
Awards: Golden Sunrise Award (West Indian World), Hansib Community Award (Caribbean Times), Achievement Award (The Business Federation), Citation (Voice Communications)

Caribbean Times, January 1994
(courtesy of Hansib Publications)

challenged me to a wager that if in any one year I was to spend £500,000 with him I could have his bat. I confidently accepted his challenge and in that same year we spent £800,000 with him. His precious trophy is now mine and takes pride of place in my collection.

Some years later, over lunch, Tony's father, Donald, admitted to me that they nearly lost the business opportunity of a lifetime simply by being bigoted. "You taught us a great lesson", he said. We became great friends and I never doubted his sincerity, but one thing for sure happened, I opened his eyes and turned his negative thinking into gold.

By this time it was patently clear that manufacturing turned out to be the company's major strength. It provided the best margins and a measure of independence in the industry. We needed therefore to try and cover as far as possible the important market segments.

Apart from expanding the Super Curl range, another brand was launched under the banner of Natural Beauty Products which had a much wider appeal and was therefore more inclusive. It carried a full cosmetics range of face powders, lipsticks, nail polishes, skin creams, soaps and lotions. The hair treatments included shampoos, conditioners, moisturisers, pomades and hair sprays. The introduction of these lines greatly expanded the company's range thus reducing the need for imported products.

In addition, a sodium hydroxide professional relaxing system was later introduced for processing the 'straight look'. The launch of this item was not without considerable difficulty. It eventually came on stream after Soft Sheen Products of Chicago bought a controlling interest in the company, which will be discussed later. The line, however, made its mark and did well, particularly in Ghana and Uganda.

Our curl products were so successful that, for a while, we experimented with a version called Curl Control under the Natural Beauty trade mark and secured two spectacularly successful shots of the curl market both at home and abroad. For a time, the brands between them dominated some markets in east and west Africa, with Curl Control dominant for years in Holland.

At this juncture, highly qualified university graduates were coming on board, and among them was Francis Okwesa, who came for an interview for his thesis in marketing. He liked what he found out about the company and the industry and later joined us as Brand Manager. He excelled in this position and brought an entirely new dimension to the company's marketing presentations, establishing our brands solidly in some of our most important markets. It is with great respect that I acknowledge his contribution.

Introduction of the universally used Afro comb under our Natural Beauty brand proved a tough endurance test in the battle of the prevailing perception that Black business was somehow bad business.

We imported huge numbers of Afro combs from the US and took a decision that we should produce a comb here in the UK under our Natural Beauty brand. This was a simple process, requiring only a mould and a slot in a production schedule. After many months approaching supplier after supplier we gave up out of pure exhaustion in finding a company willing to take on the business.

Not one to give up easily, I was still constantly on the look out for a factory that might just be persuaded to take on the assignment and as luck would have it spotted one while shopping in Wood Green.

Atlas Plastics exhibited an austere air as I approached a smartly attired uniformed guard, his brass buttons glistening in the sunshine. I explained that I did not have an appointment, but would be happy to make one to see their Sales Manager. He obliged and trotted off returning with someone who turned out to be the works foreman.

On explaining to him what I wanted, he very kindly went and brought the sales manager, a Mr Gooch, who was a most courteous gentleman who invited me to his office to discuss the project. He was quite amused with this fork-like thing called a comb which I demonstrated to him by combing my own hair. After his amusement, he agreed to my delight that he could produce the item provided we were willing to meet the tooling cost outright with a minimum first production run of thirty thousand units. I accepted his terms and invited him to provide me with a pro-forma invoice on which I will settle promptly.

We got off to a splendid start, with orders building to such an extent that they were unable to keep pace with the volume of demand that came their way. On one of my visits to the factory I asked the guard why, upon my first visit, did he bring the foreman to see me when I had asked to see the sales manager. "Well, sir," he said, "to tell you the truth, we do have a lot of Blacks working here and I thought you were just another one wanting a job."

This episode is merely another example of the perception held by many people in our society. He duly apologised and promised me he will be careful about making that kind of assumption in the future.

In the area of manufacturing, the company suffered a decisive blow in its attempt to broaden its horizon with a move into the general market place. Under our Natural Beauty brand, we contracted with Thomas Chisty & Sons of Aldershot, to manufacture for us a cocoa butter cream and lotion which turned out to be unique in skin creams at the time.

Jane Hammond of Trident Public Relations, delivered a great line in our press release of the new product line. "A beauty secret known to generations of Caribbean women was now available in the UK to pamper the delicate skins of English women, thanks to Dyke & Dryden", she wrote. Jane's message was bang on cue producing excellent feedback from our target market, the white population. Among the regular users was our bank manager's wife and daughters who loved the creams and were regularly supplied. Our generous sampling campaigns did well in creating demand, and we knew too, that we were on to a winner, for the women at the factory where the product was produced - who were all white - switched to using it in preference to what they used before.

There were two new major hurdles to cross, the first was to find a distributor with nationwide outlets, and secondly the project needed additional funding.

The return on investment in the products was good and the distributors approached expressed a willingness to take on the line provided they could be assured of regular supplies.

We were, it seemed, on the verge of a new dawn, getting into the big white market place, with what was a win, win situation, with a unique product for which there was unmistakable demand, and with distribution in place.

Sadly, our bank manager, although being involved in every detail of the project up to the point of satisfactory market testing by his own sources, still failed to finance the project. This was, without doubt, the deadliest blow of them all, and what really stunk, was that they were earning handsomely out of us.

We were devastated. Some months later, an identical product, including the wording we wrote, appeared under a different brand name which today is to be found in every high street store in the country.

Tony

A SUCCESSFUL black businessman last week attended a Downing Street reception to celebrate the country's best entrepreneurs.

The Voice, February 1984

Advertisement feature

Afro Hair & Beauty Exhibitio

Once again black businesses will take centre stage at the 13th Afro Hair & Beauty Exhibition, the single most influential event in the black hair and beauty calendar. After its successful move to Alexandra Palace, Wood Green, north London, this prestigious venue once again plays host to the annual extravaganza!

The exhibition gives exclusive access to professional hairdressers and visiting trade from 9.00 am and the general public from 12 noon - 7.00 pm on Sunday 28th May. On Monday 29th (Spring Bank Holiday) the exhibition is open to all from 10.00 am - 7.00 pm. Ticket Prices at the Door £10.00 adults, £5.00 Children & OAP's.

Unequalled in Europe, the Afro Hair & Beauty E... presents a powerful presen... under one ... stunning back drop for b... & man. 1995 sees a div... at the show, includin... clothing, confectionery, ... whom have recognised t...

Not forgetting the littl... crèche at this years Afr... For Me, (America's N... system from PRO-LINE... fantastic selection of toys... story telling and competi... will be searching for th... stylists of the future. With a ... people expected to attend over the two days, ... the

meet the hairdressers of tomorrow. Students from al... UK, will compete for the title of the Afro Hair & Beau... Student Stylist of the Year. The competition starts at... Monday 29th.

The final competition is the Afro Hair & Beauty Ph... Competition which offers hairdressers a chance to ... time. Salons submit their most creative photographs ... be judged prior to the exhibition. The winning style ... will be featured in the Afro Hair & Beauty magazine.

New for 1995 is the "Hair Alternative Show" an ev... innovative style com...

... of the "Who's who" in the industry as well as s... the world of music sport and things... glittering occa... include a

Unequalled in Europe, the Afro Hair & Beauty Exhibition presents a powerful presence under one roof and provides a stunning back drop for businesses devoted to the black woman & man. 1995 sees a diversification in manufacturers exhibiting at the show, including companies in the wine and spirit, clothing, confectionery, jewellery and travel industries. All of whom have recognised the power of the "black pound".

Not forgetting the little ones, the exclusive sponsor of the

This could so easily have been the Natural Beauty brand had our bank supported us.

The pain of this episode still haunts me, and does explain in large measure, how the banks have failed the Black community.

From the outset, it is patently clear that there was little or no risk involved whatsoever. The bank held a fixed and floating charge on all the company's assets, which at the time were two unencumbered freehold shop premises, a 16,500 sq. ft warehouse with a small mortgage and several prime leasehold properties, together with a charge on stock and debtors. We were actually held by belt and braces, for in addition to this, they also held a second charge on the directors' homes.

Despite the company's many setbacks, its manufacturing efforts have had a significant impact on employment across the wider society in many parts of the county, particularly in Yorkshire, London and Cambridge, and has helped towards building our badly needed manufacturing base.

Marketing the company's brands

WITH products of our own, a strategic marketing programme was now an absolute necessity if we were to build our brands and market share. A variety of focused marketing campaigns were put together both for home and overseas markets.

On the home front, some marketing campaigns were mostly great party occasions, full of fun with an array of young, beautiful girls eager to be selected as models or to be included in hair demonstrations. Quite apart from the social get together which these occasions provided, some saw these events as a good opportunity to get included in glossy magazines, or appearing on posters and a possible chance of getting started in a modelling career, which some actually did.

Product launches had an air of what came to be known as the "Show". Specialist choreographers would be used to pull things together. While product performance would be key, the big sell needed to be accompanied by some razzle-dazzle, which the public loved and would travel for miles to be a part of, not only for the "Show" but also for the wining and dining which followed. These gatherings were great, on-the-spot sales opportunities and our sales teams would make the most of them.

The performance of Jeff Whittiker, one of our senior sales executives, is particularly noteworthy. He was always impeccably turned out and consistently scored as top sales person in the organisation. His contribution as a team player added greatly to the company's progress and has been recognised.

One of our young rising sales stars was Jennifer Smith. She was energetic and eager to learn, enjoyed a challenge and above all was ambitious. There was, from my observations, no mistake that she would excel in a sales and marketing career. She went on to obtain a BSc and is now Product Line Co-ordinator at the Nike Corporation's European head office in Holland. We are particularly proud of her achievement.

Successful marketing methods used on the home front were soon repeated on the international stage, and Nigeria, with its huge population, became our first stop in what was to become one of many visits to that country.

Our trek took Joan Sam and myself to Ibadan to attend the first Oyo State International Trade Fair where we were hosted by my great friend Elizabeth Osinsanya, owner and Chief Executive of Elegant Twins School of Hairdressing, the oldest and most respected school in Nigeria. I record, herewith, a debt of gratitude which could never be repaid.

Elizabeth was a great host and knew all the key decision-makers and invited them to be our guests at the trade fair. The visit was a resounding success and Dyke & Dryden from then on became a household name in the industry throughout the country. Nigeria became our largest export market accounting for approximately thirty percent of our export business for a number of years. The Ibadan presentation model was requested by several distributors across the country eager to be part of the Super Curl magic.

Wherever we went, our hosts were tremendous and one in particular stood out from the rest. The Palmerson Trading Co., based in Anambra State, had exclusive distribution rights for our Afro comb, and also carried the Super Curl lines. On arrival at the airport, I was greeted with huge Super Curl banners emblazoned with "welcome". I felt like royalty and took a few days to recover from the warmth of such a reception. More surprises were to follow at my destination. A reception in my honour attended by a cross-section of the community left me speechless for a while. The offer of the traditional Kola nut as a sign of welcome and signifying friendship was passed around before the meal. During these precious moments, I reconnected with my African heritage as never before.

The next day, and with the party behind us, it was time to review our business with Mr Palmer. He expressed an observation he made that our combs were coming from a source he did not supply and enquired whether we were supplying anyone in his market. I gave him the assurance that we were not and agreed that he should investigate the matter. He promptly reported the matter to the police saying that his combs were stolen and pointed them to where they may be found. The police duly followed the lead and found some identical combs. They

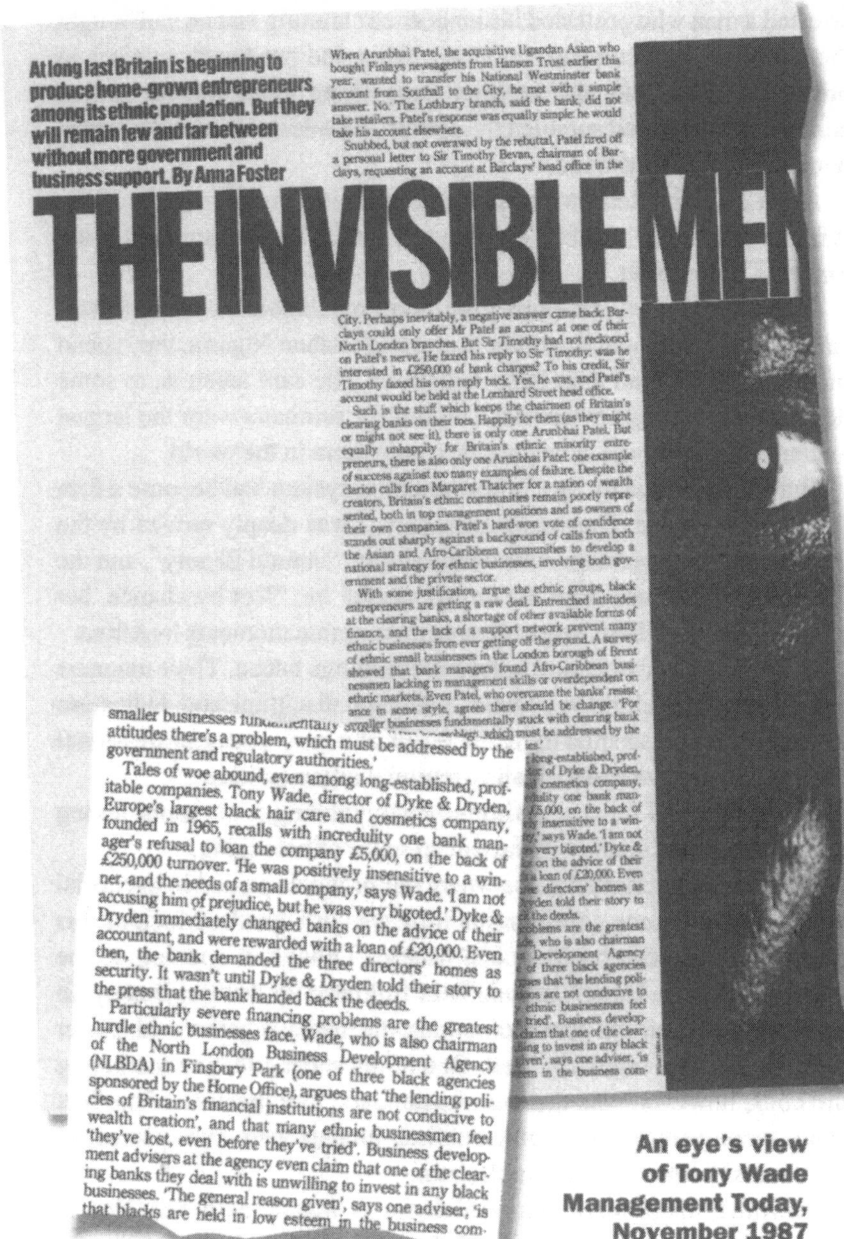

At long last Britain is beginning to produce home-grown entrepreneurs among its ethnic population. But they will remain few and far between without more government and business support. By Anna Foster

THE INVISIBLE MEN

When Arunbhai Patel, the acquisitive Ugandan Asian who bought Finlays newsagents from Hanson Trust earlier this year, wanted to transfer his National Westminster bank account from Southall to the City, he met with a simple answer. No. The Lothbury branch, said the bank, did not take retailers. Patel's response was equally simple: he would take his account elsewhere.

Snubbed, but not overawed by the rebuttal, Patel fired off a personal letter to Sir Timothy Bevan, chairman of Barclays, requesting an account at Barclays' head office in the City. Perhaps inevitably, a negative answer came back: Barclays could only offer Mr Patel an account at one of their North London branches. But Sir Timothy had not reckoned on Patel's nerve. He faxed his reply to Sir Timothy: was he interested in £250,000 of bank charges? To his credit, Sir Timothy faxed his own reply back. Yes, he was, and Patel's account would be held at the Lombard Street head office.

Such is the stuff which keeps the chairmen of Britain's clearing banks on their toes. Happily for them (as they might or might not see it), there is only one Arunbhai Patel. But equally unhappily for Britain's ethnic minority entrepreneurs, there is also only one Arunbhai Patel: one example of success against too many examples of failure. Despite the clarion calls from Margaret Thatcher for a nation of wealth creators, Britain's ethnic communities remain poorly represented, both in top management positions and as owners of their own companies. Patel's hard-won vote of confidence stands out sharply against a background of calls from both the Asian and Afro-Caribbean communities to develop a national strategy for ethnic businesses, involving both government and the private sector.

With some justification, argue the ethnic groups, black entrepreneurs are getting a raw deal. Entrenched attitudes at the clearing banks, a shortage of other available forms of finance, and the lack of a support network prevent many ethnic businesses from ever getting off the ground. A survey of ethnic small businesses in the London borough of Brent showed that bank managers found Afro-Caribbean businessmen lacking in management skills or overdependent on ethnic markets. Even Patel, who overcame the banks' resistance in some style, agrees there should be change. 'For smaller businesses fundamentally stuck with clearing bank attitudes there's a problem, which must be addressed by the government and regulatory authorities.'

Tales of woe abound, even among long-established, profitable companies. Tony Wade, director of Dyke & Dryden, Europe's largest black hair care and cosmetics company, founded in 1965, recalls with incredulity one bank manager's refusal to loan the company £5,000, on the back of £250,000 turnover. 'He was positively insensitive to a winner, and the needs of a small company,' says Wade. 'I am not accusing him of prejudice, but he was very bigoted.' Dyke & Dryden immediately changed banks on the advice of their accountant, and were rewarded with a loan of £20,000. Even then, the bank demanded the three directors' homes as security. It wasn't until Dyke & Dryden told their story to the press that the bank handed back the deeds.

Particularly severe financing problems are the greatest hurdle ethnic businesses face. Wade, who is also chairman of the North London Business Development Agency (NLBDA) in Finsbury Park (one of three black agencies sponsored by the Home Office), argues that 'the lending policies of Britain's financial institutions are not conducive to wealth creation', and that many ethnic businessmen feel 'they've lost, even before they've tried'. Business development advisers at the agency even claim that one of the clearing banks they deal with is unwilling to invest in any black businesses. 'The general reason given', says one adviser, 'is that blacks are held in low esteem in the business com-

An eye's view of Tony Wade
Management Today, November 1987

arrested a man who protested his innocence claiming that he had bought the combs from a company in Hong Kong and produced invoices to prove it. Meanwhile, the supplier from Hong Kong turned up and confirmed that he had supplied the combs. He was arrested and charged with counterfeit and fraud.

As in Nigeria, similar promotions followed in other parts of the African continent, notably in Ghana, Uganda, Kenya and to a lesser extent, The Gambia.

Ghanaian women are known for being meticulous about their hair care, and although much smaller in population than Nigeria, they spend much more per head than their neighbour. The care taken is, to some degree, like a religious fervour. Turnout for seminars were the largest and most impressive I have ever seen anywhere in the world.

Our 'Natural Beauty by Choice' relaxing system had become a firm favourite in Ghana. During the seminars, I was deeply moved by the chanting of the spectators. One would shout, "Natural Beauty", and the thunderous response from the crowd would be, "Not by chance, but choice!" For me, these were the most memorable moments in Africa.

Prayers were always said before proceedings began. Their manners and dress was a delight to witness. This rigid discipline and dedication to the profession seemed to be the result of a very strong professional culture which gave rise to healthy regional organisations.

As in Nigeria, I felt truly at home, easily relating to my roots, loving every moment of it, and feeling a deep sense of belonging.

Another major market place where our products gained in territorial dominance for some considerable time was in Uganda. Much of this fine work was done by Rose and Charles Lobago in opening up the market first with Super Curl and later followed by Natural Beauty. In addition to live, on-the-spot promotions, the media, together with poster campaigns, were regularly used. One of our most effective marketing methods, however, was the use of calendars. The practice of product shots accompanied by suitable sublime images were ever-present in customers' homes throughout the year.

The other major marketing vehicle for us was through Afro Hair & Beauty, the company's subsidiary that ran the yearly industry exhibition. More about this will follow.

Lady Pitt opening the First Afro Hair & Beauty Exhibition at the Grosvenor House Hotel

John Fashunu at the Afro Hair & Beauty Exhibition, Alexandra Palace

World Heavyweight Boxing Champion Lennox Lewis with Dyke & Dryden's Events Director Claire Jackson

Former British and Commonwealth Javelin Champion Tessa Sanderson with Tony Wade, The Mayor of Islington and Len Dyke

Dudley Dryden with his wife at Buckingham Palace, after receiving his MBE

Tony Wade with Fatou Sall, Miss Afro Hair & Beauty 1996

Tony Wade at No. 10 Downing Street with Prime Minister Margaret Thatcher

Dyke & Dryden's Events Director Claire Jackson with the late Bernie Grant MP

Super Curl Workshop in Nigeria.
Technician Joan Sam of Supreme School of Hair Design with Elizabeth Ossynsanya, Managing Director of Elegant School of Hairdressing

Press conference on the sale to Soft Sheen. (l-r) Pearl Goodridge (Dyke & Dryden's Personnel Manager), Kingsley Peter (Dyke & Dryden's Finance Director), Len Dyke, Tony Wade, Dudley Dryden and Ethan Foster (Vice President of Sales for Soft Sheen)

Judges at Afro Hair & Beauty's Battle of the Divas at London's Hilton Hotel. (l-r) Sandra Gittens (Senior Tutor, London College of Fashion), Brenda Emmanus (Television & Radio Presenter) and Oliver Skeets (former Show Jumper)

Deborah Wade making a charity appeal at Afro Hair & Beauty

Winner of the Battle of the Divas

Bishop Wilfred Wood of Croydon at Dyke & Dryden's 25th Anniversary

Battle of the Barbers at Afro Hair & Beauty 1996

Len Dyke, Tony Wade and Dudley Dryden with Bettiann and Edward Gardner, joint Chair of Soft Sheen

Pat Parkinson, Dyke & Dryden's Invoice Clerk

Rudi Page, Dyke & Dryden's Sales and Marketing Manager

Tony Wade with the late Evlyn Dyke, Dyke & Dryden's Export Manager

NLBDA delegation making a presentation to the Governor of Georgia, USA. (l-r) Judge Thelma Moore, Tony Wade, Governor Zelle Miller, Elsa Redwood, Manny Cotter, Executive Director (NLDBA) and Brian Hodge

NLBDA Board Members - (front l-r): Henry Durose, Jan Buckingham, Tony Wade. (back l-r): Dave Rigby, George Martin, Manny Cotter and Ernest Afrique

Master of Ceremonies Ralph Straker with the Mayor of Haringey and Tony Wade

The Miss Dyke & Dryden Ball, 1970

Dyke & Dryden's warehouse in north London

Dyke & Dryden's retail store in Birmingham

Dyke & Dryden's float at Notting Hill Carnival

A relaxed Tony Wade in party mood with wife Vasantha

The working environment

THE tea room, together with a shed at the back of 43 West Green Road, acted as office, work station and warehouse all rolled into one, and was home to the initial wholesale operation, while the shop front maintained its original retail status.

Tenants occupied the first and second floors which were residential and could not be used without planning permission, which took a long time in coming. Eventually, these floors became available, but it also meant carrying boxes of bottles and jars up several flights of stairs day-after-day. My legs would give up at times but my soul wanted to carry on. Many of the drivers delivering goods, would be roped into helping move the boxes up these flights of stairs. They were used to fork-lift trucks and loading bays, and would moan and swear in disbelief on seeing where their deliveries had to go. As leader of the pack, there was no escaping this back-breaking exercise. I had to be out in front, encouraging them all the way, and at the same time conscious of weight and the risk of the boxes coming through the ceiling.

A temporary short term answer was found by buying a nearby building at 126a West Green Road which helped to reduce the storage problem. However, this created another problem, that of moving goods between the two sites. Addressing this unworkable situation was a high priority. Estate agents were approached to assist in finding suitable premises, and a 5,500 sq. ft facility was found at 10 St Loys Road about a mile from our original location. This was a welcome relief and sense of much satisfaction to all concerned. State of the art equipment was purchased which made loading and unloading less of a headache and made the working environment as a whole a far more desirable place.

The move to St Loys Road was another turning point. This was ideal, providing space to move about, with all stock at eye level which made order filling far more simple, resulting in faster turn around times for gathering and packing orders.

This respite, however, was short-lived, for we had grossly under estimated our space requirement, and two years later, had out grown the warehouse. Fortunately, our agents found us a 15,500 sq. ft purpose-built building at 19 Bernard Road which we purchased in 1982.

Our new premises provided us with a superior working environment, a proper kitchen and canteen together with excellent office accommodation to cope with the various departmental functions of personnel, accounting, sales and marketing, which grew in line with the needs of the business. In addition, and for the first time, there were decent offices for the directors.

Another superb spin-off to occur from this location, was the opening of a cash and carry facility where hairdressers and traders could purchase stock directly. This innovation made a difference and improved the company's cashflow.

The immediate, all round gains in efficiency were remarkable and boosted productivity to levels never seen before. Progress continued apace and, inadvertently, Bernard Road became the meeting place for everyone connected with the industry. Different visitors had different objectives. The American manufacturers, for example, were keen to ensure that they were still getting their fair share of distribution space and at the same time monitoring our manufacturing efforts which, after all, were now competing with them. And there were those who wanted to enter what was now a lucrative business niche and wanted to copy our methods of operation or buy into the business.

Manoeuvring through the many demands placed on us as a result of the company's success, became a delicate balancing act in deciding which direction we should take. After much soul-searching, both Len Dyke and Dudley Dryden decided to sell their interest in the business.

The fight with officialdom

AT every level of our development, we seemed to, somehow, come up against situations which became a problem for us while others in the same industry, and in identical circumstances, were left alone.

In this instance, it concerns our local VAT officers who were distastefully threatening and were it not that we were financially sound, they would have brought upon us financial ruin.

Export sales were a significant part of our business and thus zero rated. VAT Office guidelines state that Certificates of Shipping must be produced as evidence of export which we followed to the letter.

In some instances, however, customers would nominate their own shippers who we would accordingly deliver to as directed with a certified delivery note and corresponding invoice. Once the goods were transported, the shipper is obliged to furnish us with a valid Certificate of Shipping.

It turned out that some shippers took instructions from our mutual customers and included with our merchandise on the shipping certificates in some instances "household effects" and on others "personal effects". On discovering this irregularity we approached the shippers and demanded certificates showing exactly what we delivered to them.

The shippers explained that they took instructions from the people paying their freight bills, but were prepared to confirm receiving and shipping the goods received from us, adding that they could not see what the fuss was all about as they do this all the time with no problems what ever.

Unfortunately for us the VAT officers would not budge, they refused the shippers confirmation and insisted that we pay up. The matter went before the commissioners who upheld their officer's demand for several thousand pounds. We could only conclude that we were clearly less favourably than others in the same situation and the unanswered question remains why?

In one of many meetings with the officer inviting him to show some understanding of the circumstances surrounding the case, he was green with nothing but envy, remarking that "you boys could pay" - he had just read about the company at 10 Downing Street."

Dyke & Dryden Travel

THE travel service side of the business grew out of popular demand and persuasion by many of our loyal customers who insisted that they preferred doing business with us and would welcome our efforts to handle their international travel arrangements.

This exceedingly high regard with which the company was held could not be taken lightly and steps were taken to meet their demands resulting in the establishment of an agency to service their needs.

For a while, as with all of our other associated businesses, Dyke & Dryden Travel operated from 43 West Green Road, squeezing use out of every square inch of the building. Looking back it is quite amazing how we improvised to make things happen in what was less than five hundred square feet of space.

In time, the travel business obtained its own premises with the purchase of 93 West Green Road. From here it operated as an independent business unit with its own staff and overheads. Although we shared the overall management of the company as a whole, the day-to-day running of Dyke & Dryden Travel was entirely the province of Len Dyke.

The purchasing of airline tickets represents large sums of money and it was necessary to always exercise great care in its handling. Len was most particular about this, especially when it came to the movement of cash between the office and the bank. He had good reason to be cautious following an attempted daylight robbery at the office after customers had paid in substantial sums of money that day. Fortunately, the robbers were inexperienced and were scared off by the arrival of other customers.

The agency prospered and expanded its activity in line with the growing demand at the time for charter flights by residents in the UK returning to visit their relations and friends back home in the Caribbean, especially at Easter, in the summer and at Christmas time.

Charter flights were organised and operated through 'members clubs' which offered its members privileged club fares. There were a number of well known and respected clubs, among the best known were the Jamaican Overseas Families & Friends Association (JOFFA), the Barbados Overseas Families & Friends Association (BOFFA), the West Indian Overseas Nationals Association (WIONA), and the Inter-Caribbean Social Club run by Dyke & Dryden Travel.

Between them, these clubs pioneered a unique way of substantially reducing the cost of travel back home and were the envy of large carriers like British Airways who had a virtual monopoly on flights into the Caribbean at regular scheduled fares only. By working together the clubs were able to charter their own aircraft and pass on the benefits to the members while retaining reasonable management fees and expenses.

This arrangement worked well for several years until some dishonest organisers became involved in the industry, and many travellers fell victim to their scams. As a result, new legislation was introduced which ruled out the clubs and required bonded travel consolidation and special operators' licences. While this change in the law effectively got rid of the cowboys, it also penalised the legitimate clubs.

Some Caribbean travel agents with IATA and ABTA accreditation have to some extent only themselves to blame for missing out on obtaining consolidators' licences by their failure to find a framework in which to operate together and share in the current mass movement of people across the Atlantic.

The Caribbean is today one of the world's fastest growing holiday destinations, and the hope remains that before long our travel agents will eventually become major players in this lucrative market.

A further area of growth in the market is to be found in the large numbers of returnees who, after reaching retirement age, have chosen the sunshine of the Caribbean in preference to the cold of Europe. In addition, some have built strong English, European and inter-island friendships and have become regular visitors thus expanding the market further.

With the loss of the travel club system and increased demand on management time with the other sectors of the company, Dyke & Dryden handed over the travel side of its business to colleagues in the industry. Our involvement has been rewarding not only from a profits stand point, but also in providing a service to thousands of people who placed their trust in us.

Afro Hair & Beauty

FOUNDED in 1982, Afro Hair & Beauty was soon to become Dyke & Dryden's marketing arm, the vehicle driving the industry in the UK and opening up the market across Europe.

Rudi Page, our Sales and Marketing Manager, with his youthful enterprise, was asked to take the lead in the task of liaising with potential exhibitors, exhibition contractors, hairdressers, fashion designers and models, and to work with Jane Hammond of Trident Public Relations, our PR company, in pulling things together. Rudi coined the name 'Afro Hair & Beauty' which aptly describes what the exhibition was all about.

Dyke & Dryden had organised the first trip to the Bronner Brothers Show in Atlanta for Black hairdressers and retailers. It was the model on which Afro Hair & Beauty was based. As a reward for his performance the previous year, Rudi was sent on a trip where he made the best use of his visit by observing the steps to follow.

Afro Hair & Beauty is an organisation dedicated to the education, development and promotion of the ethnic hair care in Britain, and it remains the shop window of the industry.

What does it mean in economic terms? It means self-employment and independence for thousands of people in a variety of ways. There are over one thousand salons across the country, employing an average workforce of three - more than three thousand jobs. On the retail front there are more than two thousand stores selling our products, employing an average of two to three people which means a further six thousand jobs. In addition to these, there are hairdressing schools, manufacturing and distribution outlets, also employing significant numbers.

If we were to add the attendant services of management, accounting, sales and marketing, one will quickly see the multiplier effect on employment as a whole, and just how profoundly it affects the lives of so many families.

The company's first exhibition, held at the prestigious five star Grosvenor House Hotel in Park Lane, was a trail-blazing affair, welcomed by the industry and public alike. This was a brave step by the hotel and ourselves as neither of us knew exactly what we were getting into.

Black people and their friends responded to the press and radio commercials and came in their thousands, eager to see at first hand what this new and exciting happening was all about.

For the first few hours, the sheer numbers were a cause for concern that we may be unable to accommodate everyone and disappointment would be a source of trouble. I was gratified that my fears were unfounded. The crowd behaviour was marvellous from start to finish. There were lots of shouts of, "well done, it was about time we had our own show".

Jane Hammond of Trident Public Relations did a splendid job in creating national and international awareness, filling the venue to capacity and was duly credited for a job well done.

Lady Dorothy Pitt, the darling of the community, and a great supporter of Black enterprise, performed the opening ceremony paying a fitting tribute to all the participants from home and those who travelled from overseas. She declared that the event represented a major landmark in Black pioneering history and enterprise. She reminded the gathering that "Black is beautiful and we must never be tired of saying so or showing how true that is". Her remarks were prophetic, for with eighteen years behind it, the exhibition has been a cornerstone in building Black enterprise in the UK.

American companies saw the exhibition as the shop window for the industry in Europe and the ideal platform for expanding their businesses this side of the Atlantic. They were lavish with concentrated high profile promotions which captured the imagination of everyone who attended the event. The media had a field day and commented favourably on the merits of this new development.

The exhibition has had an enormous influence on the development of many small ethnic businesses and the expansion of several medium-sized companies providing a sizeable number of jobs in its wake.

Afro Hair & Beauty became part of our community development policy, by always allocating a number of free stand spaces to small,

The Post Entrepreneural Profile

TONY WADE, MBE.

major black-business landmark within the U.K.

The Dyke & Dryden story is one that conjures up feelings of admiration and pride in those that come to hear it. It has all the ingredients of grit, determination and guts, that we've all come to expect from any company of people, who would do something that society has come to expect, is rarely done by a given particular set of people. As a black-owned company, surely it is something for the whole black community to be proud of ? And a blue-print for many of the business-minded amongst us, to try and emulate in the future.

Tony Wade has been central in this particular story. The plight of both the man and company, are stories about the kind of drive and determi[nation] that you need in o[rder to sur]vive and do well

The Post, May 1999

new business start-ups, enabling them to display their goods, services and skills in several different disciplines. These included people in the fashion and design industry, in the performing arts, film making, music and dance routines.

As the fame of the event grew over the years, visitors came from all over the world and so making an impact on the local economy by pushing up occupancy levels of our hotels, checking out our fine restaurants and famous stores.

The role of the event has been widely recognised at all levels of the establishment, and visited by government ministers, Members of Parliament, civic leaders, captains of industry and celebrities from stage and sport.

While its central plank is business centred, it is also packed full of fun and is a great day out for the whole family. Creativity is high on the agenda, adding tremendous value for the community.

Competitions such as 'Battle of the Barbers', where the barber sculpted wild and wacky designs; for style diva of the year, hairstylists demonstrated their creativeness for day or evening styles in the 'Battle of the Divas'; and the 'National Free-Styling College Competition' for the young budding hairstylist to exhibit their originality. The 'Avant Garde Hair Competition' extravaganza gave the opportunity for stylists to give free reign to their imagination. In addition, fashion and hair show presentations by many of the exhibitors combined to launch many young and up-and-coming hopefuls. Some went on to become household names, such as Celetia, Cruz and Truce in music and fashion.

Highlight of the weekend was the 'Miss Afro Hair & Beauty Competition' (sponsored by Air Jamaica), an integral part of a charity ball with the proceeds going to charities such as NCH Action for Children, UNICEF, the African & Caribbean Leukaemia Trust , the Sickle Cell Society and the Caribbean Mental Health Association. Spirited auctions at the event by the effervescent Garth Crooks, reigned in the bidding with items supplied by celebrities such as Lennox Lewis and others, and Tessa Sanderson, Patrick Agustus, Saracen, Victor Romero Evans, Janet Kay and others gave generously of their time in the support of the many good causes named above.

Clair Jackson, Events Director for ten years, who has been a central pillar in the organisation, says, "I look back on my years spent as Events

Director of Afro Hair & Beauty Exhibition as a period of great joy and challenge". Clair was extremely hard working, conscientious and perceptive and has made a most valuable contribution to the product of Afro Hair & Beauty.

The vibrancy of the event continues to educate and excite, attracting its patrons like a magnet from around the world. It remains a great outing for the entire family in the Black social calendar, and if you are young at heart, you can't afford to miss the Afro Hair & Beauty After Party.

Catering for the many thousands who make the annual pilgrimage to Alexandra Palace is always a sought-after contract for keeping the massive crowds well fed and watered, and is in itself one example of how the event helps to develop the community from within.

The employment opportunities generated by the event are considerable and includes a number of annual contracts for activities such as stand building and design, lighting and electrical fittings, around-the-clock security services, scores of hair and fashion models, show presenters, press and public relations consultants, cleaning services, car park attendants and many others, which adds up to a formidable army of workers.

For a time, the Miss Afro Hair & Beauty Ball was the place to be seen at, and attracted many Black women all vying for the coveted crown which carried several super prizes along with fame for the winner. Sponsorship for the exhibition over the years was provided by Dyke & Dryden and has been a powerful marketing tool for the company which helped immensely in building its image and bringing its products to the attention of the public.

Len Dyke, Dudley Dryden and myself are gratified in seeing the fulfilment of the objectives for which the exhibition was founded.

There is little doubt about the influence and impact it has had on almost every sphere of life across the country - from food to music and fashion, including the introduction of the heart-warming colours of the Caribbean, facts which hopefully will be reflected in the future social, cultural and sociological history of Britain.

The sale to Soft Sheen

IN November 1987, a change in the ownership of Dyke & Dryden occurred which was to chart a new path for the company. My two colleagues, Len and Dudley, felt it was time to slow down and agreed to sell their shares to Soft Sheen Products, a Chicago-based corporation which was the leader in the ethnic hair industry with sales approaching US$100 million.

As it happened, both companies came from similar backgrounds, sharing an almost identical philosophy of using their best endeavours to contribute in building a Black economic base within our respective communities. Surprisingly, many voices in the UK Black community expressed their unhappiness that control was lost to the Americans. For the record, I must let it be known that long before the sale across the Atlantic was even considered, a conscious effort was made to divest the shares within the Black community in the UK. Unfortunately, those who showed an interest were faced with the old difficulty of being unable to raise the necessary capital.

The rationale behind the marriage, at the time, made good business sense and offered new horizons with huge potential benefits for both parties. It made Black business history - two Black companies linking up across the Atlantic was something that had never happened before.

The media and the industry were rife with speculation about the deal, and waited anxiously to see the direction in which the new management would take the company. Their anxiety was understandable, as both companies were leaders in their respective markets, the competition felt threatened.

It was during one of my marketing excursions in Nigeria, where our brands were among the leaders, that I met with the President of Soft Sheen who expressed his interest in purchasing the business if we were to consider selling.

On my return to London, I duly communicated the news to Len and Dudley and from there on the wheels were put in motion to do a deal which took eighteen months to conclude. During this time, the news of the proposed sale was leaked and attracted several offers, with one US company flying in on two occasions by private jet and offering over and above our asking price in an effort to secure the business. Their offer was not accepted.

It may seem senseless to the reader that we did not accept the best offer, and with hindsight, this was perhaps un-business like, but our commitment to Black business development was such that cash was not our only consideration at the time.

The Americans gloated about the acquisition, and in a press statement declared that, "by buying into Europe's largest distributor they have stolen a march on their manufacturing competition by profiting from them through their subsidiary". This was a colossal error of judgement for which Dyke & Dryden was later to pay the price.

This boast infuriated the competition, bearing in mind that Dyke & Dryden was a master distributor and carried the competition's products as well as its own. The response to that inept statement was immediate and severe.

The first shots from our once good friends, was to squeeze Dyke & Dryden's supplies, while others refused to supply us at all. This was merely the beginning of the chaos that was to follow. Seconded management from Chicago came ill-prepared, without the faintest idea of the dynamics of the European market place and, worse still, were not prepared to listen.

Soft Sheen, as already mentioned, was the largest player in the industry and the pre-acquisition, grand master plan, in brief, had three elements to it. The first was to use Dyke & Dryden's distribution network across Europe and Africa to dominate the market; secondly, to expand the retail chain in the UK as a first step, and then move the Dyke & Dryden brand into other countries; and thirdly, to expand and build the brands already owned by the company.

On paper these were wonderful visionary aspirations. The International Director who was to implement the plan was equally bullish in his briefings with staff, raising the level of expectation for a meteoric take off.

First steps were to harmonise our computer systems and introduce modems with head office in Chicago to enhance the many benefits linking up would bring with it.

In December that year, Kingsley Peter, our Finance Director, and I visited Chicago to meet with our opposite numbers in the new set-up. The most pressing item on the agenda was the replacement of our current computer for an IBM36. Kingsley, under whose portfolio this came, wanted, quite rightly, to make the purchase in the UK for ease of service and other practical reasons which I supported. The Soft Sheen people, on the other hand, insisted on using the people they already worked with in the States. A compromise was, however, eventually reached, that we would purchase the hardware in the UK, and they would purchase the software in the States. This was our first major disagreement and it brought home to me, for the first time, the loss of my executive decision-making role.

As predicted, accessing and fitting the software presented nothing less that chaos. The equipment was inoperable for well over a year and ran up costs of just under £100,000. Kingsley's frustration boiled over on this and other related issues and as a result resigned his position with the company.

This bungling had cost the company its most valuable member of staff. He was a first rate Finance Manager who had served the company well with his exceptional accounting skills. His position, today, as Area Financial Controller for National Grid - one the UK's top one hundred businesses - is proof of his calibre.

Kingsley's replacement was sent from head office, rather than recruiting in the UK and, needless to say, it was another inept decision over which I had no control or input.

It was patently clear that the seconded staff were not up to the job, and were letting down the organisation. Their reports to Chicago were misleading and did not reflect the realities on the ground.

Despite this colossal daily pressure, I never lost my nerve, and simply summoned up that reserve of inner strength which situations like these call for. I could not have done otherwise, for I was still the Managing Director, if in name alone, to whom everyone looked for a solution.

Eventually, an independent audit was ordered which stated, "it is our impression that the position of the Managing Director has been obscured by the involvement of Soft Sheen personnel in the day-to-day management of the business. Overall responsibility for decision making no longer appears to vest in the Managing Director, but to be diffused between Soft Sheen, the Managing Director and Soft Sheen personnel working at the company. The result is that the company lacks clear direction, and decision making is a protracted and inconclusive process."

In the face of this unbelievable turmoil, my response was to offer to buy back the company, and made an offer to Soft Sheen in 1994 which was rejected. In September the following year, however, a deal was struck and the company reverted back to me - though all the poorer by approximately £1 million.

In any event, although the marriage did not work out as planned, it would be true to say that the intentions of the principals on both sides were honourable and defeated only by short-comings on implementation.

Important lessons have been learned, and the message from Gary Gardner at Dyke & Dryden's 25th Anniversary, quoted below, holds true for every generation of Black entrepreneurs across the world.

"Black enterprise both in Britain and the United States is still in its infancy. The future promises an increasing number of Black entrepreneurs, capable of achieving the commercial success, that Martin Luther King spoke of, many years ago as the route to equal rights.

Dyke and Dryden and Soft-Sheen are two notable examples of what can be achieved, when determination and hard work meets a market need.

When in 1987 Soft-Sheen took shares in Dyke and Dryden, a partnership began that united two completely complimentary business philosophies, and an element of social responsibility and community work, that is rare in today's business environment.

We look forward to developing both the commercial and social interests of Black people internationally and working through established and new business partners alike."

A STORY OF SURVIVAL

DYKE AND DRYDEN LTD 1965-1990

In May 1965 Dyke & Dryden was founded with the opening of a small retail shop in West Green Road, north London. The founders, Len Dyke and Dudley Dryden sold records and cosmetic products. Mr Dyke ran the business while Mr Dryden continued with financial support earned from his trade as a carpenter. On May 26 1990, twenty-five years later, with 3 retail units, 2 cash and carry warehouses, a wholesale department, a 24 hour service distribution department and a 'brands' department, Dyke & Dryden Ltd celebrate their 25th Anniversary.

A Rare Breed

In the aftermath of the 1958 race riots in Notting Hill and Nottingham, life was tough for black people in Britain, and to find a place to live was almost impossible. Renting premises to set-up shop called for a rare brand of determination and character.

Dyke and Dryden who were also founding members of the Westindian Standing Conference WISC, (set up as a result of the troubles), had those qualities.

Attending regular WISC meetings and encouraging people to stand up for their rights and seek economic strength, meant that when the opportunity came along to get started in business, Len and Dudley practised what they had been preaching.

Obstructions and objections

In the second year of business there was a serious cash-flow problem, and the bankis total lack of support made life extremely difficult for the business. When Dudley Dryden went to his branch to ask for a 'facility' he was told by the manager that he was iwelcome to lose his own money but not the bankisí He had to go out and tie up his life insurance policies as security.

Len Dyke was in no better shape with the bank manager to whom he had been recommended. The manager insisted that Len sell his small family property in Jamaica to raise capital.

The partnership became a company in 1968, when Tony Wade, a credit controller, joined Len and Dudley. The three directors decided to retain the trading name Dyke & Dryden.

A second retail unit was open in Ridley Road, a street market in east London, in spite of racist objections and amid a steady flow of obstructions from the other traders. Ridley Road street market was becoming very popular with the local Westindian community.

Charter Flights

The company also ran a charter flight and shipping service to the Caribbean and North America from the West Green Road unit. In 1971 Dudley Dryden joined the company full-time.

Dyke and Drydenís Record and Cosmetic store, which from the beginning, has been the leader with 'pre-release' (Ska, Blue Beat and Calypso) records, founded a recording company called Double D Records. By 1973, the music business had become so cut-throat that Dyke and Dryden Ltd decided to close that part of their operation and concentrate on the cosmetic side of the business.

In the early days most Westindians came to this country with a plan to stay a minimum of 3 years and a maximum of 5 years. Then with enough money, return home and start-up a business

The obstacles were enormous. The three directors who took less wages than when they had been employees, struggled on with the support of their families and eventually sound business strategy succeeded in establishing Britainís first national black business.

The move in 1975 from the company's 3rd unit, a 5000 square foot wholesale department to an 11,000 square foot warehouse, was due to an increase in nationwide retail and export sales.

The 'Ploy' that failed

Having acquired three units 36-40 Ridley Road by 1975, Dyke and Dryden were suddenly shocked to

Dudley Dryden MBE, Tony Wade MBE and Len Dyke

discover via the local newspaper that planning permission had been granted by, Hackney Planning Department to British Rail to locate a new railway station on the exact spot where the 3 units stood.

The news was devastating, there would be no compensation and no possibility of relocating in Ridley Road. There had been no consultation by either the local council or BR.

This was easier said than done and Mr Dryden spent weeks and later months going from shop to shop and stall to stall seeking campaign support. He did manage to get about 50 per cent of the Ridley Road traders behind the protest and after two tense and near exhausting years, BR withdrew their application and Dyke and Dryden breathed a great sigh of relief.

The irony of the experience was that BR reopened the railway station in Kingsland High Road, which had been closed since 1850, and which was less that 500 metres from the street market site where the Dyke and Dryden units were located.

At the time of possible closure, Dyke and Dryden was the only black business in Ridley Road ... was it a political 'ploy' to get them out? There seems no logic behind the proposal to locate a BR station in the middle of the street market.

The Big Wide World

In 1983 the company moved their present enlarged office, warehouse and distribution centre and in 1987 as a result of commercial and social interests were joined in a business venture by the US company Soft Sheen. The company is now gearing up for a major thrust into Europe, Asia, Africa, the Westindies and the Arab countries where they have been widening their sale base.

"The music in particular was a great marketing exercise, people from black home wanted to keep up with the latest music and they knew we could get it for them".

At present Dyke and Dryden have over 700 different products from 40 brands. The most significant sales coup was made in April 1990 when the Boots chain took on board Dyde and Dryden products. This gigantic leap into high streets of Britain and Europe is a significant achievement for the pioneers of black cosmetics in Britain.

Community Involvement

Along the course of Dyke and Drydensí history one constantly finds tremendous community involvement. Time spent in work for the community has been seen as an investment... the foundation of the companyís success.

Regarded by many as the only source of help, in hundreds of instances, the directors have shouldered responsibility and responded to the needs of others. The community and society have acknowledged the efforts of the directors and awarded the MBE to Mr Dudley Dryden and Mr Tony Wade (Mr Dyke is on the waiting list). Hundreds of other awards, including the prestigious Hansib Community Awards, have been made to all the directors and the company itself.

Afro Hair and Beauty Show

Another area of achievement has been the Afro Hair and Beauty show, which will take place at the Kensington Town Hall.

Caribbean Times, May 1990
(courtesy of Hansib Publications)

The buy-back from Soft Sheen

THE power of positive thinking was, for me, always a major strength and really nothing less could have prepared me mentally for the mammoth task that lay ahead in rebuilding the business. I told myself that I did it once before, and could do it all over again.

Confident in my belief, a restructuring plan was immediately triggered. This entailed getting right back, as it were, to basics by stripping out of the organisation all its unproductive elements. With decision-making now back where it belonged, there was no one to answer to about how to use the pruning knife.

I was never given to ruthlessness, though I really should have been, given the behaviour of some members of staff who abused the trust placed in them to the detriment of company's survival. They were, however, seen off appropriately and will forever have to live with their consciences.

Staff reductions to the bare essentials was a first step, followed by lopping off the retail segment of the company. Some units were sold to members of staff on easy terms, while others were sold to outsiders. The wholesale and general distribution followed in similar fashion, leaving the company free to focus on its most profitable segment, the manufacture of its brands.

Our new direction was communicated to the industry, and from there on it was simply a question of managing change, driven by one objective, that of restoring the financial health and respect of the company.

The challenge was formidable, but certainly achievable as long as we stayed focused on the goals that we had set ourselves, and to that end, a new energetic and experienced manager was found to implement the company's new direction.

My new management team, led by Tony Goodridge, an accountant, had under his belt years of experience in the industry and knew most of the customers well. His mastery of creative accounting and relationship management kept every one happy until we were in a position to deal with our creditors.

The other cog in the new team was my personal assistant and confidant Claudia Newton. She was a first class all rounder providing me with support far above the call of duty and I will always be indebted to her super contribution in restoring the health and pride of the company.

Confidence returned once the industry received the news that I was back in the driving seat. It was truly a source of comfort finding that my many industry friends held me in such high esteem, for which I an extremely grateful.

Funding the turnaround was, fortunately, not too difficult a process which simply meant turning one of the company's unencumbered freehold properties into cash and with prudent and tight accounting policies we were well on the way, and discovering new horizons for the business.

A new and imaginative marketing campaign was launched to coincide with the 1996 Afro Hair & Beauty Exhibition, Dyke & Dryden's subsidiary through which a clear and positive statement was made to our many customers and the industry at large.

The market response to our new vibrant colour cosmetics range designed by the Beauty Bar, went down like a treat with ladies of all ages and shades. The 2-in-1 foundation was in particular a big hit, and in the words of our consultants, Noella Mingo-Jones and Allison Edwards, "we demystify but don't dictate".

Our brands that have stood the test of time were enhanced and improved in most areas with the introduction of the Natural Beauty four application kit, now a firm favourite with the professionals.

At this juncture, I cannot help but revisit the circumstances already mentioned which gave rise to the development of the company's brands, for as it turned out, our brands ultimately became the cornerstone of our survival in a market that had matured with time.

Being hands-on once again, infused a new sense of exhilaration, a new freedom to explore and be creative which is, in essence, I believe, at the heart of all achievement and turning negativity into gold which, for me, has been a joyous experience with a soft landing.

Dyke & Dryden and the community

DYKE & Dryden has been a community business right from the start, kindling that "can do" spirit which somehow seemed to have been evading the vast majority of the Black community in the UK at the time.

Music as a launch pad for the business could not be more appropriate, for it provided that missing 'something' which was an intrinsic part of our culture, the enchanting rhythms of ska, soul, blue beat and calypso. These were sounds which most West Indians grew up with and loved, and a store where these treasures could be found was a paradise where people could meet and share each other's music and company, engendering a sense of togetherness which the power of music like nothing else transmits.

House parties in the late Fifties and early Sixties were the most popular mode of entertainment, and people would travel from near and far to buy the records they loved, passing on the news to their friends and directing them to Dyke & Dryden who built a special kind of relationship with the public.

This historical relationship remained a harmonious one throughout, the company being ever mindful of its own painful beginnings, and provided community support wherever possible.

Our people pay a heavy price for their absence in the higher rungs of management through failure on the part of most employers to promote people with proven skills and ability. Quite often highly qualified persons are passed over for promotion in favour of less qualified staff with less experience.

Indisputable evidence exists to confirm this very disgraceful treatment of so many people within our community, and while the position is marginally better now, there remains a long way to go in addressing this situation.

We pride ourselves on good relations with our staff and our provision for them of a healthy and happy environment. There was an unspoken assumption that the company belonged to the community. Our staff never suffered the distress and indignity of being by-passed for promotion by their inferiors as was the case with many white-owned companies.

Influencing change is, however, by far the most significant of all the benefits that have accrued to the community as a whole. In the first place, it has become a role model for thousands of our people, creating that "can do" attitude which is so necessary if, as a people, we are to succeed. In the second place, it provided a seed bed for the development of a range of skills, training and managerial experience which were to benefit the individuals and their families, the community and the economy as a whole.

There is a further important economic dimension to this community self start effort, which brings into play the multiplier effect with several past members of staff who are now business owners and managers in their own right engaged in wealth creation and further extending the enterprise culture.

Seeing the spirit of enterprise flourishing among past members of staff is a source of great satisfaction. Names such as Clarendon Ventures, Afrique, Headlines, TZ Enterprises, Statecraft Consulting and Supreme all came out of the Dyke & Dryden stable and are positively engaged in the business of wealth creation, which for me is a source of great joy.

The comments of Veronica Williams are a further good example of community networking:

Treasured Moments, a florist business offering creative displays with exotic flowers and plants, started trading in 1995. We had approached a number of British companies to offer our services, but it was our relationship with Dyke & Dryden that gave us the opportunity to be the floral plant contractor at the Afro Hair & Beauty Show which springboarded our company. From this relationship, further doors were opened to magazines and newspapers such as Black Beauty & Hair, Pride, The Jamaica Gleaner, and Caribbean exhibitions such as Jamaica Expo. Victoria Mutual Building Society, Lusters, Fashion Fair, Choice FM and others including various bridal shows, were among some of the many and varied companies and venues that have used our services in providing floral and plant displays over the years.

In addition, many young people who wanted to follow a business career were always welcomed for discussions and advice. Several students for example, did their thesis on the company, while others did so on the industry.

Another area of company community involvement was the offer of placements, enabling graduates to gain experience in their effort to find employment in the wider society. It was a common complaint by many newly qualified persons that they were often refused employment because of lack of experience.

Influencing change had also in its sights, the bigger picture of bringing to the attention of senior managers in the establishment and captains of industry, their responsibility to take a lead in ensuring that their organisations were not merely paying lip service to equal opportunity, but needed to show by their actions and employment practices where they stood on this issue.

The opportunity for me to do so came in a number of ways. First by example, for although a relatively small company with staff numbers averaging between forty five and fifty five persons, our make up was a mixture of all races. This was a positive statement around which there was no escaping for employers who could not subscribe to our example.

My involvement on boards both in the private and public sectors provided opportunities to put across some of the issues affecting our community. One such organisation was Business in the Community whose membership included many heads of some of the country's largest businesses, of which Prince Charles is President. As it happened, I was co-opted onto the Governing Council of this body by the then Chief Executive, Stephen O'Brien, a man blessed with a double helping of energy. This body does sterling work particularly in the inner cities, with members of our community benefiting from its work in many ways.

Dyke & Dryden itself was a beneficiary of the organisation's work by way of its membership and ability to network. An outstanding example was our chairman's intervention on our behalf which resulted in our success in getting our products into the Boots Chemists chain.

All three directors already engaged in public life were to become further involved. Len Dyke chaired the West Indian Standing Conference for some considerable time and later put in time with prisons, immigration, and currently serves as a Mental Health Act Manager

BLACK BEAUTY

Serving the community

Dyke & Dryden celebrate their 25th anniversary this year. *C&D* meets three "founding fathers" of Britain's black haircare industry to chart their progress, and their operations director, who outlines company philosophy for the '90s

Twenty-five years ago Len Dyke and Dudley Dryden were two men with a vision. Both were founder members of the West Indian Standing Conference, an umbrella organisation set up in 1958 against a background of racial disturbances, particularly in London. The aims were to bring together a number of smaller groups to "preserve the spirit of Caribbean unity" to strive for social, political, cultural and economic aspirations, and to foster racial harmony.

But it was the pursuit of economic independence that, in 1965, gave birth to Dyke & Dryden. Len Dyke left his job as an electrician with British Rail and pooled resources with Dudley Dryden, a carpenter, and took out a [illegible] Green [illegible]

Dyke & Dryden celebrate their 25th anniversary this year. *C&D* meets three "founding fathers" of Britain's black haircare industry to chart their progress, and their operations director, who outlines company philosophy for the '90s

[illegible] out the [illegible] to become in those [illegible] rare to see a black business and everyone was very proud." To repay the community for their support the two started to concentrate on the hair care field, where very few products were available.

In 1968, they were joined by Tony Wade, now managing director, and the trio started to look overseas, importing cosmetics from America and Jamaica. Records sales and the travel business were phased out and the retailers set their sights on supplying other specialist shops and market stalls then springing up around London.

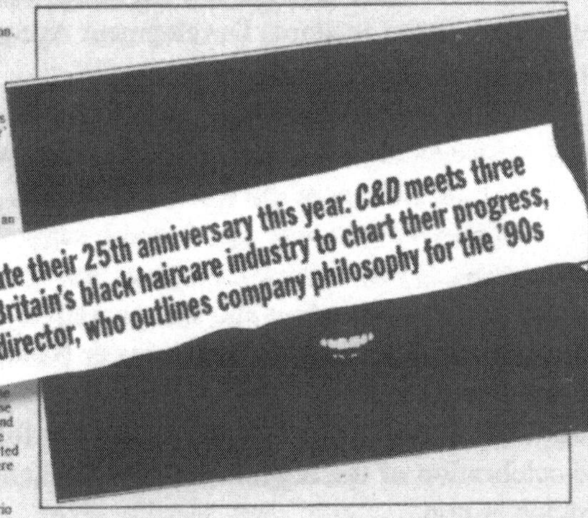

Wholesale development

"The wholesale and distribution business grew out of the retail operation with us breaking bulk on imports. We started supplying food shops and hairdressers with pressing oils and curling wax for ladies and pomades and hairdressings for men," says Tony Wade. Products were distributed from a storeroom at the back of the shop but expansion of imports led to the need for larger premises, resulting in a move further down West Green Road.

From supplying brands like Sweet Georgia Brown, Madame Walker and La India in the late '60s, Dyke & Dryden grew to become agents for major American companies like M & M, Soft Sheen and Carsons, in the '70s.

"We were pioneers in the industry. Many of the major brands were launched through Dyke & Dryden who bore the cost of advertising," says Mr Wade.

In 1971 the Natural Beauty budget make up range was launched, and ten years later, the Supreme Super Curl hair care products, both "own brand" UK-manufactured ranges.

In 1983 the company moved to their current premises in Bernard Road, Tottenham, a 17,000 sq ft warehouse and office site, with over 40 employees. 1983 also saw the birth of the Afro Hair & Beauty show, an annual event which has grown to be the largest of its type outside the US.

And in 1987, history was again made when America's largest black hair care manufacturer, Soft Sheen, acquired a 66 per cent stake in Dyke & Dryden. "It was a great achievement, linking up with a company in the States with which we'd been doing business for a long time," explains Mr Dyke.

Pharmacy gives support

Independent pharmacies have always been supportive of the black hair care business and have played a big part in its development, says Mr Dyke. But many make a fundamental mistake, by not giving adequate shelf space to ethnic hair care, warns Mr Wade. "Black people are shoppers by habit and there is high brand loyalty. If they see what they wanted on display it would improve trade enormously. Give pride of place to the needs of your black consumer," says Mr Wade.

Messrs Dyke and Dryden are now both non-executive directors of the company. When they arrived in England in 1955, their plan was to work for five years, save some money and return to Jamaica. But like many others they stayed and are still here serving the community with dignity.

Chemist & Druggist, April 1990

with the Haringey Mental Health Trust, London, dealing with patients' appeals.

Dudley Dryden also worked with the Conference holding various offices. He did some fine work as Vice Chairman of Hackney Race Relations Council and served as a liaison officer with the police. His skills in human relations was widely respected and honoured in 1984 with an MBE.

In my case, much further public related work was to follow. After the Scarman Report following the Brixton uprisings, the government acted on its recommendations and my name was put forward to chair the North London Business Development Agency (NLBDA), one of three initiatives in the London region.

This role involved much time away from the business and needed careful consideration with my colleagues after which we all agreed it would be time well spent and that I should do it.

The agency's remit was as the name suggests, to assist with the development of small ethnic businesses and was funded by the Home Office with match funding and sponsorship by a number of leading companies such as National Westminster Bank, Allied Lyons, Shell Oil and others.

As Chairman of the NLBDA, I made the following statement at the celebration of the organisation's tenth anniversary, held at the London Hilton:

Clocking up ten years of sustained achievement in an organisation like our does call for a celebration! Of much more importance, though, is our history and the circumstances that gave rise to our existence.

Ten years ago, some of us responded to a call from Sir Leon Britton, the Home Secretary at the time, to implement some of the recommendation of Lord Scarman's report following the Brixton riots. Before attempting to summarise what we have achieved over these past years, perhaps it would be helpful to look at the broad objectives we had been set.

Our first task was to increase the level of preparedness for ethnic people wanting to enter business by way of advice and counselling as a first step within our local community. Secondly, to work with new and existing businesses and assist in finding start-up capital and

10 VOICE May 24 1994

Changing the face of Stonebridge

Stonebridge estate is a notorious housing estate with a long history of crime, but all that is set to change under a new government-based programme. A Housing Action Trust (HAT) is destined to give the area a much-needed face lift. *Anthony André* investigates

TONY WADE: Set to lead the Stonebridge project

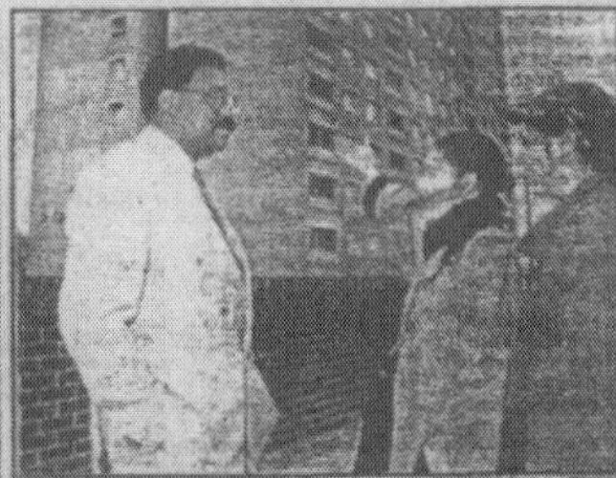

CLIVE LLOYD: Shadow deputy chair

Stonebridge is a stereotypical inner city housing project of the type constantly featured in dramatised [illegible] series, where the repetitive droning of a distant hi-fi can be heard echoing through the cold inhospitable dirty grey concrete slabs that 1,700 families call home.

This rundown, crime ridden, inner city council estate could be considered as the blot on a council copy book – a place where, in recent years, [illegible] have been [illegible] for local police. [illegible]

Wall-to-wall graffiti and patches of green grass add a touch of [illegible] colour to this otherwise depressing configuration of human habitation. For those who dwell there, Stonebridge is the predominant factor in their lives, heavily influencing their prospects of a brighter [illegible].

According to locals, if you're applying for a job the last thing you want to say is that you live there.

Usually, the people who have been housed there come as a last resort. It is the final frontier where people fear to tread unaccompanied. But all that is about to change.

On March 14, the residents of Stonebridge voted with a two thirds majority in favour of the massive Housing Action Trust (HAT) regeneration programme, set up by the Department of the Environment under the 1988 Housing Act. Estimated to be worth a staggering £100 million over ten years, the scheme will take [illegible] out of local government control.

[illegible] per cent of the 1,[illegible] eligible voted in the secret ballot. Of this number, 68 per cent ([illegible]) voted in favour of the HAT and 32 per cent ([illegible]) against it. If the dissenters had won the area would have remained under local council control.

But the HAT programme should not be interpreted as a case of throwing money at an "unsightly blemish" of the past, say its supporters. It is more than that.

Tony Wade MBE, a well-known successful Black businessman, has been appointed by the government to lead the proposed HAT urban regeneration scheme for the run down north London estate.

Achieve

He said: "From what I have seen of Stonebridge I am convinced that a HAT is the right solution. A HAT is unique in providing guaranteed funding, the principle of real consultation with residents and a commitment to improving job prospects and community facilities."

Mr Wade added: "Nobody consulted the people of Stonebridge when the estate was constructed some 25 years ago. To achieve real and lasting improvements the community has to, and will be, involved."

[illegible]

> **NIGERIAN FAMILY? SETTLED IN ENGLAND?**
>
> *Laurence would like to as well*
>
> 
>
> Lawrence (5 years) needs a black adoptive family who can offer him a permanent, secure home and promote his racial and cultural background. He is Nigerian and of the Yoruba tribe and Christian. He has no contact with any of his family who are in Nigeria.
>
> Lawrence's early life was not very settled but for the past two years he has been living with a foster family. Lawrence is a healthy, good tempered, intelligent child with a lovely smile. His foster mother says he is considerate, sunny natured and likes the company of other children and adults. He is proud of his appearance and loves dressing up for parties. Lawrence likes school and is popular. He is used to children and needs a family with one or two parents. There should be a gap of at least two years between him and other children. If you think you could help Lawrence and would like to find out more, please contact:
>
> **Val Reed on 071 932 0635 or 976 6211 x2236**
>
> or write to: *Family Placement Service/2nd floor, Ebury Bridge*

The Voice, May 1994

guidance as appropriate. Thirdly, to develop working partnerships with central government, local government and the private sector to stimulate the enterprise culture and Black business development in general.

How have we fared over the years? Our public accountability reports have shown both measurable and quantifiable results of which we could be justly proud. We have succeeded in translating objectives into actions, action into facts and facts into statistics. Our business initiatives have moved from being local to national, and from national to international involvement on behalf of our clients, and the NLBDA is now an established resource centre in our areas of work.

In all this, we are conscious that we have done little more than barely touched a tiny part of the huge task of bridging the gap of sharing in the economic life of our nation. Racial disadvantage is fuelled, in the main, by the level of unemployment among ethnic communities, and the only effective response is the pursuit of fair and equal opportunity if the notion of a "One Nation" battle is to be won.

All the evidence we have collected points to some key facts. The need for ongoing education and training in business management, re-skilling in all areas of activity and access to finance is critical to the development of the Black community, enabling it to be more productive and self supportive. Failure to do so will only serve to perpetuate poverty for generations to come.

The Black community's willingness to work hard and contribute must be recognised, and to that end, under representation of ethnic participation in national economic life, is not so much an ethnic problem alone, it is a national problem for our country as a whole.

Ethnic business development must be seen in the context of an investment in the UK's economic future, and I urge everyone in a position to influence this process to do so. Partnership is one of the ways forward and, indeed, the NLBDA is itself a product of partnership.

On behalf of our board, our Executive Director, Manny Cotter, and his staff, may I offer our sincere thanks and appreciation for the formidable support we have had for all our sponsors and supporters over the last ten years.

POSITIVE STEPS?

THE Greater London Council Industry and Employment Committee has decided on an eight-point plan to help black business development and black community enterprises.

Michael Ward, Chairman of the Industry and Employment Committee said: "We are recognising as a priority that black businesses here have special problems. They find it harder to get finance. They find it harder to get sound business advice. They find it harder to get the kind of premises of viable business needs.

"A recent survey showed almost all ethnic minority enterprises are in back street locations away from main roads or busy shopping centres, which starts by loading the dice against their commercial success.

"Despite their declared interest in helping black businesses get access to finance, only one of the major clearing banks has appointed a development officer for black business in inner city areas so far, and the difficulties remain.

"The council wants to assist black businesses in a number of ways. As a start we want to set up a Black Business and Community Enterprise Development Working Group involving minority groups and statutory interests to guide our activity in this field."

"We shall also encourage the GLC Supplies Department to consider, through its role as a larger purchaser of both goods and catering contracts, how to encourage ethnic minority enterprises."

The initiatives suggested in a report to the Industry and Employment Committee and now agreed include:

* Providing grants to assist with start-up capital costs.
* Providing grants to cover interest costs on start-up loans.
* Making appropriate Council-owned buildings available where possible and practicable.
* Asking local planning authorities to consider the race relations implications when they consider applications from black businesses and community enterprises.
* Inviting local authorities and bodies such as the New World Business Consultancy and the UK Caribbean Chamber of Commerce to submit business development proposals and community enterprise initiatives for consideration by the GLC.
* Supporting black organisations providing comprehensive business advisory services.

Mr. Tony Wade Chairman of the UK Caribbean Chamber of Commerce welcomed the GLC's proposals. He said this was the most positive initiative for the community in a long time and said it was the beginning of real help.

Tony Wade ... welcomes GLC's proposals

Peter Tucker - Chief Executive Commission for Racial Equality.

I warmly welcome the GLC's initiative, since my recent visit the USA. I have advocated for the development ,of Bl Businesses and we at the CRE are ourselves actively interes in the matter. I hope that other authorities and agencies follow the GLC's effort.

Caribbean Times, 21 May 1982
(courtesy of Hansib Publications)

Time spent at the North London Business Development Agency was a resounding success, delivering well over three thousand business start ups with a survival rate above the national average. Several of these businesses are today significant employers and wealth creators in the local economy. One good example is Benjamin Oswald Transport Ltd, a business currently employing some 40 employees.

By this time, Soft Sheen had become the majority share holder in Dyke & Dryden and they too agreed that my public work should continue and it was just as well that they did, for somehow I became a candidate for other related work which my experiences were now attuned to.

Another bold new government initiative was unfolding across the country to put in place the Training and Enterprise Councils which were to stimulate enterprise, improve training skills and educational standards. The make-up of the boards of management for the TECs had to be at managing director or chief executive level with two thirds from industry. Again, I found myself being nominated for the Board which covered Haringey, Enfield and Barnet where I served for ten years after which I resigned in June 1999.

I must have been doing something right, for invitations to serve on other bodies kept coming my way, without any attempt on my part. The next appointment to follow was for a three-year spell with New River Health Authority, serving the Boroughs of Enfield and Haringey where I served as a Non-Executive Director for three years.

This work was very rewarding in many ways, for in this position, certain recommendations I made were introduced which brought about significant changes for the better in the management of the Authority. The Board expressed its gratitude by inviting me to stay on after the end of my contract but I was unable to do so, for yet another challenge presented itself, one where I believed I could make a difference.

Stonebridge Estate, comprising some 1,750 dwellings and 5,000 inhabitants in the London Borough of Brent, was one of poorest inner city areas characterised by poor housing, high unemployment, and all the many social evils associated with it. The Council, unable to finance the rehabilitation of the estate applied to central government for Housing Action Trust status to deal with the problems of the area and succeeded in getting it.

In early 1993, I was one of several candidates interviewed for the post of Chairman for a non governmental body to deal with the redevelopment of Stonebridge, and I was the successful candidate, appointed by Sir George Young, the Housing Minister in November 1993.

The brief was to redevelop or refurbish the estate, improve the management and maintenance, improve the social conditions by way of job creation through training, and by improvement in community and leisure facilities.

This was a project that had to be taken right off the ground and with the secondment of Lucy Robinson, an exceedingly able civil servant from the DoE, and an initial budget of £100 million pounds, we were up and running. Lucy and I made a great team and delivered what was expected of us during our tenure of office.

Contribution on the business front at the national level is equally noteworthy. In February 1984, the company was one of thirty seven businesses invited to 10 Downing Street by the Prime Minster, Mrs Margaret Thatcher to celebrate the country's best entrepreneurs.

Again, on 5 November 1985 at the British Overseas Trade Board Conference at the Barbican, Dyke & Dryden was one of five companies selected by BOTB in their marketing campaign, "The world is your market", aimed at encouraging small and medium size companies into exporting. One third of our sales were in export markets.

Working with young people as a Director of the Princess's Youth Business Trust, east London branch, was very rewarding in helping to encourage, inspire and point them in the right direction. Other work with youth, and equally satisfying, was to serve as a Member of the Corporation of the College of East London and being part of the decision-making of the college in providing a quality education for our students.

The company, through the efforts of its directors, has come a long way in helping our community to position itself in many responsible roles in the society in which we live and work, and represents what I hope is merely the beginning of a page in Black British history.

The current government has boldly nailed its colours to the anti-racist mast. The decent people in Britain have been looking for this courageous leadership. This approach gives me great hope for the future. An equally encouraging signal too, was the appearance of the Leader of the Opposition at the Notting Hill Carnival sharing in the joyous celebration of an event which now truly belongs to the nation as a whole.

During an interview with Hugh Scully on Nationwide in the Eighties, one of the questions I was asked, was what in my opinion was holding back the Black business community. There were three situations I explained as I saw it. There was in the first place, the lack of access to capital, secondly the absence of the opportunity for managerial experience by the failure of employers to promote Black people in the work place who qualify for promotion, and thirdly, that our community had a weak political leverage.

Without doubt, there has been some improvement in all three areas, with the most significant on the political front according to a recent survey carried out by Operation Black Vote. This survey shows quite clearly that the ethnic community holds the balance in determining what could happen in some one hundred parliamentary constituencies.

I regard myself as a bridge builder, and reject the politics of militancy and confrontation and hope that our new found strength in this area will help to ensure a more fair and equitable partnership in all our national endeavours, and have been consistent in my belief of the virtues of co-operation.

I am happy to note in my observations, that our people refuse to wallow in self-pity, anger or bitterness. They are getting on with the job of carving out a better future wherever possible for themselves, relying on the priceless gifts of hard work, discipline and resourcefulness, insisting only on equal opportunity, freedom from fear, and equality before the law.

In my speeches to business and other related bodies, I have pointed out from time to time, that it is not only governments which should be righting wrongs, be it gender, race relations or class discrimination. Other influential sectors too, have vested interests as exemplified by the Diversity policy of General Motors one of the worlds largest corporations.

John Smith, GM President, sums up its quintessential rationale thus: "In our industry, as in this nation, diversity is our strength. This diversity is more than a part of our national pride. Having people of widely different ethnic, racial and social backgrounds in our corporation has not slowed our pursuit of excellence – it has accelerated it."

It was good to hear our Prime Minister echoing these sentiments in his Birmingham speech not so long ago after the senseless outrage by the doers of evil in our society.

In my business experiences since 1968 I have learnt that diversity is good for business, and I hope that through these pages more people will embrace Diversity as others have already done.